ST. BERNARD'S SERMONS

ON THE

BLESSED VIRGIN MARY

ISBN 0 85172 736 0

2nd impression, September 1987

Printed by
MASLANDS LTD., TIVERTON
and published September 1987 by
AUGUSTINE PUBLISHING COMPANY,
CHULMLEIGH, DEVON EX18 7HL.

ST. BERNARD'S SERMONS

ON THE BLESSED VIRGIN MARY

TRANSLATED FROM THE ORIGINAL LATIN

BY

A PRIEST OF MOUNT MELLERAY

DEVON, MCMLXXXIV

CONTENTS

I

FIRST SERMON ON THE GLORIES OF THE VIRGIN MOTHER

" The Angel Gabriel was sent from God into a city of Galilee, called Nazareth,
" To a virgin espoused to a man whose name was Joseph, of the house of David : and the virgin's name was Mary "—Luke i. 26-27.

Why, it may be asked, does the Evangelist in this passage mention by their proper names so many persons and places, and that with such evident deliberation ? It is, I believe, because he wishes to remind us of the attention with which we should peruse what he is chronicling so carefully. He names the messenger who is sent, the Lord Who sends him, the Virgin to whom he is sent, and even the spouse of the Virgin. He also designates by their proper names the family of both spouses, their city, and their country. Wherefore this ? Shall we suppose that the inspired author has set down anything without special signification ? Surely not. For if a leaf falls not from the tree without cause, if a sparrow does not " fall on the ground without (the permission of) the Father " in heaven, how is it credible that a superfluous word could flow from the lips of the holy Evangelist, especially whilst he is narrating the sacred history of the Incarnate Word ? No, I cannot believe it. On the contrary, I affirm that everything here is full of heavenly mystery, every smallest detail abounding in divine sweetness, yet only for him who examines it with diligence, and who knows how to " suck honey out of the rock and oil out of the hardest stone." For, as the Prophet Joel predicted," on that day the mountains

1

dropped down sweetness and the hills overflowed with honey and milk," when the heavens "distilled dew from above and the clouds rained down the Just," when the exulting "earth opened and budded forth a Saviour," when "the Lord gave benignity and our earth yielded her fruit," when on that Mountain of mountains, on that "curdled and fat Mountain," "mercy and truth met each other, justice and peace embraced." At that time not the least among the other mountains, viz., the disciples of Christ, was this blessed Evangelist who, in mellifluous language, tells the entrancing story of the origin of our salvation,—a veritable aromatic hill, which of old under the warm breath of the south wind and from the vicinity of the radiant Sun of justice, exhaled and diffused abroad the sweet odour of its spicy treasures. Oh, that now also God would vouchsafe to "send out His word and melt" for us these spiritual spices! That "His wind would blow," in order to liquefy and make intelligible to us the odoriferous words of this Gospel narrative! That He would place them in our hearts as a rich inheritance, "more to be desired than gold and many precious stones, and sweeter than honey and the honeycomb"!

The Evangelist therefore says, " The Angel Gabriel was sent from God." I do not suppose that this Angel belonged to the inferior choirs of blessed spirits who are frequently sent to the earth on embassies of ordinary importance. An evident reason for thinking so is furnished in his very name, because " Gabriel " signifies " Strength of God." Another reason is the fact that he is not said to have been sent by any higher angel, as is usually the case when the heavenly messenger happens to be of inferior dignity,* but directly by God Himself. It is therefore with the design to insinuate this that the Evangelist is not content to say, " He was sent," but adds, " from God." Or perhaps the addition is made lest we should think that God revealed His counsel to any even of the celestial court before it was made known to the Virgin,† excepting of course the Archangel Gabriel, who was found so highly exalted amongst his fellow-spirits as to be accounted worthy of so glorious a name and of so honourable a mission. And his name accords well with his mission. For how could anyone more fittingly announce Christ, " Who is the Power of God," than he who has been honoured with the similar name of " Strength of God " ? What difference is there between the Power of God and the Strength of God ? Nor ought it to seem improper or unbecoming that the messenger should be called by the same name as his Master, since that name is not applied to both with the same signification. For Christ is called the " Power " or the " Strength of God " in a sense in which such a title cannot be understood of the Angel.

---

* That is to say, the lower angels ordinarily learn the divine decrees which concern themselves, not immediately from God, but by illumination from the higher spirits : just as on earth the divine will is made known to us through human superiors. Cf. St. Thomas, *Sum. Theol.*, I. q. cvi. a. 1-2 ; cf. also Suarez, t. ii. l. vi. c. xii.-xv —(Translator).

† But how could the angels have been ignorant of what was known to the patriarchs and prophets ? The Saint solves this difficulty (de Bapt. v.) by distinguishing between the substance of the mystery and its circumstances. That the Word was to become incarnate the angels knew from the beginning, but as to the circumstances of place, time, mode, and persons, they, like the prophets, had no clear knowledge. Somewhat similar is our own knowledge of Christ's second coming, as St. Bernard himself points out. In this position the holy Preacher is supported by St. Thomas, I. q. lxiv. a. 1 ; and by Suarez, t. ii. l. v. c. 6, n. 33 —(Translator).

The name " Strength of God " as applied to the Angel is purely titular, whereas in Christ it is not a name simply, but a name that expresses His Nature. He is what He is called, the " Power of God," Who coming with superior strength upon " the strong man armed " that was wont to keep his court and his possessions in peace, " overcame him " by the might of His arm, and forcibly took away from him his captives and his spoil. But the Angel is named the " Strength of God," not because he possesses in himself the reality signified by this name, but either because he merited to obtain the high prerogative of being chosen to announce the coming of Him Who is the true " Strength of God " ; or else because it was his duty to comfort the Virgin, naturally timid, simple, and retiring, lest the announcement of so unheard of a prodigy should overwhelm her with fear : hence we find him reassuring her with the words, " Fear not Mary, for thou hast found grace with God." We may suppose, and not without reason, that it was the same Angel who comforted her humble and modest spouse also, saying to him, " Joseph, son of David, fear not to take unto thee Mary thy wife," although in recording this incident the Evangelist does not mention the Angel's name. Gabriel, therefore, was most fittingly chosen to herald the Saviour's coming ; or rather he is most fittingly designated by this name because chosen for so high an office.

" The Angel Gabriel," then, " was sent from God." But whither ? " Into a city of Galilee, called Nazareth." Let us see whether, as Nathanael says, " any thing of good can come from Nazareth." The word " Nazareth " means " a flower." Now, it seems to me

that the celestial communications and promises made
to the fathers, to Abraham, to Isaac, and to Jacob,
were, in a sense, the seed of the divine counsel, cast
from heaven on the earth. Of this seed Isaias says,
" Except the Lord of Hosts had left us seed, we had
been as Sodom, and we should have been like to
Gomorrha." It attained to florescence in the wonders
which were wrought " when Israel went out of Egypt,"
in the figures and signs exhibited throughout the whole
long journey across the desert to the promised land,
afterwards in the visions and predictions of the prophets, and finally in the institution and government of
the kingdom and the priesthood, down to the Christian
era. Christ Himself may be properly understood to be
the Fruit of this seed and of these flowers. Hence the
Royal Prophet sang, " The Lord will give goodness,
and our earth shall yield her Fruit." And again,
declaring God's promise to himself, " Of the Fruit
of thy womb I will set upon thy throne."
Christ therefore is announced to be born in Nazareth,
because we naturally expect to see the fruit coming
forth from the flower. But when the fruit has made
its appearance, the flower falls off ; so too, all types
and figures vanished away as soon as Truth appeared
in the flesh. Hence also Nazareth is said to be a
" city of Galilee," that is, of " transmigration " (such
being the meaning of the name Galilee), because at the
birth of Christ all those things which I have just
enumerated and which, as the Apostle declares,
"happened to them (the Israelites) in figure," passed for
ever away. Indeed we can see for ourselves we, who
are now enjoying the Fruit, that the flowers are all
withered and gone. And even whilst they were still

in bloom it had been foreseen that they should perish. This may be inferred from the words of the Psalmist, " In the morning it shall grow up like grass, in the morning, it shall flourish and pass away ; in the evening it shall fall, grow dry and wither."* For " in the evening," that is to say, in the evening of the world, " when the fulness of time was come (and) God sent His Son, made of a woman, made under the law," proclaiming, " Behold I make all things new " : in that evening, I say, all the types and shadows of the old dispensation passed away and disappeared, just as the blossom falls and withers when the new fruit comes forth.   Therefore it is also written, " The grass is withered, and the flower is fallen : but the Word of the Lord endureth for ever."   It will be granted, I suppose, that the Word here stands for the fruit.   Now the Word of the Lord is Christ.

Christ is, consequently, the excellent Fruit That " endureth for ever."   But where is the grass which has withered ?   Where is the flower which has fallen ? Let the Prophet Isaias answer : " All flesh is grass, and the glory thereof as the flower of the field."

But if " all flesh is grass " and if " the grass is withered," it follows that the nation of the Jews, since they are carnal, must be withered as the grass. Can we doubt that this people are withered, whilst we behold them, strangers to the sweet unction of grace, obstinately adhering to the dry and sapless letter ? And is not their flower also fallen, since the glory which they derived from the law has been lost to them for ever ?   But if that flower still remains, where, then,

* This is only an accommodation, for it is clear from the con-text that the Prophet is speaking of man —(Translator).

is the kingdom ? where is the priesthood ? where the prophets, and the temple ? where those mighty wonders of which they used to boast, saying, " How great things have we heard and known, and our fathers have told us," and also, " How great things He commanded our fathers that they should make the same known to their children " ? This is all I have to say in connection with the words, " Into a city of Galilee, called Nazareth."

Therefore the Angel Gabriel was sent from God into this city of Nazareth. But to whom was he sent ? The Evangelist informs us, " To a virgin espoused to a man whose name was Joseph." And who is this Virgin, so venerable that she is saluted by an angel, yet so humble that she is espoused to an artisan ? We have here a beautiful alliance of virginity with humility. And surely that soul must be highly pleasing to God in which humility commends virginity and virginity adorns humility. But what degree of reverence shall we not judge her to be worthy of whose humility fruitfulness glorifies, and whose virginity is consecrated by motherhood ? You have learned that she was a virgin and you have learned that she was humble. If you cannot imitate the virginity of the humble Mary, at least imitate the humility of the virgin Mary. Very desirable is the virtue of virginity, yet humility is more necessary. We are counselled to embrace the former, but the latter is a matter of precept. To the one we are invited, to the other we are constrained. Concerning virginity the Saviour only says, " He that can take it, let him take it " ; whereas He speaks thus of humility : " Unless you be converted and become as little children you shall not

enter into the kingdom of heaven." The first, there
fore, is commended with the promise of a special
reward, whilst the second is exacted as a debt. One
can be saved without virginity, but without humility
salvation is utterly impossible. The soul that is humble,
I say, even if she has to lament the loss of her virginity, may nevertheless be pleasing to God; but—I
dare to affirm it—the virginity even of Mary would
have no value in His eyes apart from her humility.
Hence He has said by His Prophet Isaias, " Upon
whom shall My Spirit rest but upon him that is humble
and quiet ? " * Notice that it is not on virginity He
has promised that His Spirit shall rest, but on humility.
Consequently, had Mary not been humble the Spirit
of the Lord would not have rested upon her. But if
He had not rested upon her, He would not certainly
have made her fruitful. For how could she have conceived by Him without His co-operation ? It is
evident then that, as she herself declares, God " hath
regarded the humility of His hand-maid " rather than
her virginity, in order that she might conceive by the
Holy Ghost. But although she was pleasing on account of her virginity, still it was her humility that
made her a mother. And hence it may be said
that her humility was the true reason why the Lord
took complacence in her virginity.

What sayest thou to this, O proud virgin ? Mary,
forgetful of her virginity, glories only in her humility,

* This reading of Is. lxvi. 2, differs considerably from the
Vulgate, which is thus rendered by the Douay Translators :
" But to whom shall I have respect but to him that is poor
and little ? " The Septuagint differs from both : " ἐπὶ τίνα
ἐπιβλέψω, ἀλλ᾽ ἢ ἐπὶ τὸν ταπεινὸν καὶ ἡσύχιον;" " (To whom shall
I have respect but to him that is humble and quiet ?)—
(Translator).

and dost thou, on the contrary, applaud thyself for being a virgin whilst taking no pains to become an humble virgin ? " He hath regarded," she says, " the humility of His hand-maid." Who is she that speaks thus ? She is a virgin, and a virgin conspicuous for sanctity, for prudence, and for piety. Dost thou pretend to be more pure than she ? or to be more pious ? Perchance thou believest thy chastity to be more pleasing than was Mary's, and that thy virginity will be sufficient of itself, and without the help of humility, to win the favour of God, whereas her's was not ? Oh, consider that the more honourable thou hast been made by the singular grace of chastity, the greater is the injury thou dost inflict on thyself by thus befouling thy beauty with the filth of pride ! In truth, it were more expedient for thee to have lost thy virginity than to make its preservation a reason for pride.* Virginity is a virtue that is found with few, but far fewer are they who combine it with humility. If therefore thou be one who can only admire the virginity of Mary, apply thyself with zeal to copy her humility, and that will be enough for thee. But if thou art both a virgin and an humble virgin, thou hast attained to true greatness, whosoever thou mayest be.

Nevertheless, there is something further for thee to admire in Mary, something even more wonderful than this union of humility with virginity. I refer to that prerogative by which she unites integrity with fruitfulness. For " from the beginning of the world it hath not been

---

* Similarly St. Augustine : " Superbis continentibus expedit cadere, ut in eo ipso in quo se extollunt, humilientur " (Ser. 65 De Verbis Domini) —(Translator).

heard that any " woman was at one and the same
time a mother and a virgin. And oh ! if thou remem-
berest Whose Mother she was, what bounds shalt thou
set to thy admiration of her incomparable grandeur ?
Shalt thou not be brought to understand that thou
canst never admire her as much as she deserves ? Shall
not she who has God for her Son be exalted in thy
judgment, as in the judgment of Truth, above all
creatures, even above all the choirs of angels ? Is not
the God of the universe and the Lord of the angels
called Son by Mary, who, as the Evangelist St. Luke,
tells us, once said to Him, " Son, why hast Thou done
so to us ? " Which of the celestial princes would dare
to use such language ? It is enough for them, yea, it
is a great thing in their estimation, that having been
created pure spirits, they received from grace the
dignity and the name of angels of God. Hence the
Psalmist says, speaking to the Lord, " Who makest
Thy angels spirits." But Mary, remembering that she
is His Mother, gives with confidence the name of Son
to that awful Majesty Whom they are happy to serve
with lowly reverence. Neither does the Lord disdain
to be called what He has not disdained to become.
For a little further on the same Evangelist from whom
I have last quoted tells us that " He (Jesus) was
subject to them," viz., to Mary and Joseph. God
became subject to man ! God, before Whom the
angels prostrate, Whose commands are carried out by
the powers and the principalities, that God, I say,
was subject to Mary, and not to Mary alone, but to
Joseph also, for Mary's sake ! Admire therefore these
two marvels, and choose which of them thou wilt
admire the more, whether the gracious condescension

of the Son, or the glorious exaltation of the Mother. Each of them oppresses our mind, each of them passes our comprehension. That God should obey a woman is a condescension without parallel ; that a woman should command God is a glory beyond compare. Where the Evangelist is speaking in praise of virgins, he mentions it as a special prerogative that " they shall follow the Lamb whithersoever He goeth." Of what praise, then, shalt thou deem her worthy, who follows not but precedes the Lamb ?

Learn, O man, to obey ; learn, O earth, to bear the yoke ; learn, O dust, to be submissive. It is of thy Creator the Evangelist is speaking where he says, " And He was subject to them," namely, to Mary and Joseph. Oh, be ashamed, proud ashes ! God humbles Himself, and dost thou exalt thyself ? God subjects Himself to men, and dost thou, by striving to subject men to thee, prefer thyself to thy Maker ? Would to God that, whenever such ambitious thoughts possess my soul, I might hear addressed to me the words in which the Saviour once replied to the Apostle who had rebuked Him, " Go behind Me, Satan, thou art a scandal unto Me, because thou savourest not the things that are of God, but the things that are of men " ! For as often as I entertain the desire to rule over men, so often do I endeavour to run before God. Then truly I do not " savour the things that are of God," of Whom it is written that " He was subject to them." O man, if thou disdainest to follow the example of man, surely thou wilt not deem it a dis- honour to imitate thy Creator. And if thou art not able to follow Him " whithersoever He goeth," at least refuse not to follow Him whither He condescends for thy sake. I mean to say, if thou canst not follow Him in the sublime way of virginity, follow Him, follow thy God in the safe path of humility, from the straightness of which should any one wander, even though he belong to the number of the virgins, such a one, to confess the truth, does not " follow the Lamb whithersoever He goeth." The proud virgin does indeed follow the Lamb, and so too does the humble penitent ; but neither follows Him whithersoever He goeth, because whilst the latter cannot ascend to the purity of the Lamb Who is without spot, the former is equally unable to descend to His lowly meekness, Who was dumb not only before His shearers, but even before His slayers. Nevertheless, the penitent soul that follows Him in the path of humility has taken a safer course than the proud soul that imitates His virginity. For whereas humble satisfaction shall wipe away the stains of the one, the purity of the other shall be tarnished by her pride.

But how happy is Mary, to whom neither humility is wanting nor virginity ! Hers, moreover, is a singular virginity, which her fruitfulness has not injured but enhanced ; just as hers is an unparalleled humility, which her fruitful virginity impaired not but glorified ; aye, and her fruitfulness also is incomparable, attended and adorned as it is by humility and virginity. In which of these qualities is not Mary wonderful ? in which is she not pre-eminent ? in which not unique ? I shall be very much surprised if, in balancing them, one against the other, thou art not puzzled to determine which is the most worthy of thy admiration, whether thou shouldst feel greater wonder at the fruitfulness of the virgin than at the integrity of the mother; at her exaltation in her Son, or at her humility in the midst of such glory. But undoubtedly all these, taken together, are more marvellous than any one of them ; and it is an incomparably better and happier lot to have received the whole of them than some without the others.

And what matter for surprise is it that God, Who is said and Who is seen to be "wonderful in His saints," has shown Himself still more wonderful in His Mother ? O all ye who are engaged in the married state, look with admiration on this incorruption of the flesh in corruptible flesh ! Ye consecrated virgins, wonder at this alliance of virginity and motherhood ! Children of Adam all, imitate the humility of God's Mother ! And do you, O holy angels, honour the Mother of your King whilst you adore the Child of our Virgin, Him Whom both you and we acknowledge as our Sovereign Lord, Who is the Redeemer of our race and the Restorer of your city. To the Same, therefore, so sublime with you in heaven, so humble with us on earth, let us all unite in showing the reverence which His Majesty requires, and the honour and glory which is due to His condescension both now and for evermore. Amen.

II

SECOND SERMON ON THE GLORIES OF THE VIRGIN MOTHER

" The Angel Gabriel was sent from God into a city of Galilee, called Nazareth,
" To a virgin espoused to a man whose name was Joseph of the house of David, and the virgin's name was Mary "—
Luke i —26-27.

No one will question that that new canticle which only virgins shall be permitted to sing in the kingdom of God, shall be sung by her who is the Queen of virgins, as well as by the others, aye, and that she shall take the lead in singing it. But it seems to me that besides this canticle, in which, though proper to virgins, yet all the virgins, as I have said, shall join with their Queen, there is another more sweet and sublime wherewith she alone shall rejoice the city of God. No one else, even amongst the virgins, shall be found worthy to utter and express the sweet-sounding modulations of this second song. The right to sing it shall be reserved, and justly, to her alone, who alone of virgins glories also in being a mother, and in being the Mother of God. But although she glories thus, she does not glory in herself, but in Him Whom she has brought forth. That is to say, she glories in the Lord Who has made Himself her Son, and Who, having prepared for His Mother a singular glory in heaven, willed also to endow her on earth with a singular grace, whereby, in an ineffable manner, she might conceive without stain and bring forth without corruption. For the only nativity worthy of God was that which made Him Son of the Virgin, just as the only maternity

worthy of the Virgin was that which made her Mother
of God. Now, when the Creator of men willed to become
man and to be born in the human way, it was necessary
for Him to select, or rather to create for Himself, out
of all possible women, such a Mother as He foreknew
would be worthy of Him and deserving of His esteem.
He therefore decreed that she should be a virgin, from
whose immaculate womb He would issue forth immaculate, in order to cleanse all others from their stains.*
He likewise decreed that she should be humble, so that
she might worthily give birth to one Who is meek and
humble of heart, and Who was destined to exhibit to
the world, in His own life, a necessary and most salutary
example of these two virtues. Therefore, He who had
before inspired her with the will to make a vow of
virginity,† and had also endowed her with a singular
grace of humility, now caused her to experience the
joys of motherhood, whilst remaining still an immaculate
virgin. For how could the Angel pronounce her *full*
of grace (as is read further on) if she possessed any,
even the very least good, which was not the fruit of
divine grace ?

Thus she who was destined to conceive and bring
forth the Saint of saints, obtained the grace of virginity in order that she might be " holy in body," and
the grace of humility that she might also be " holy in
spirit." Adorned, therefore, with these gems of the
virtues, all resplendent with this double sanctity of
body and spirit, the Royal Virgin " by her comeliness

* " Voluit itaque esse virginem de qua immaculata imma-
culatus procedere, omnium maculas purgaturus."
† The same opinion is expressed by St. Augustine, *Lib.
de sancta Virginitate* c. iv. According to St. Thomas (*Sum.
Theol.*, III. q. xxviii. a. iv.) the Blessed Virgin took this vow
after her espousals and with St. Joseph's consent —(Translator.)

and her beauty " became an object of admiration to
heaven, attracting to herself the wondering eyes of its
citizens, and even inclining the Heart of the King to
desire her beauty ; with the result that she was visited
from on high by the celestial ambassador. This is
what the Evangelist intimates, when he tells us that
the Angel was sent from God to the Virgin. " The
Angel Gabriel," he says, " was sent from God into a
city of Galilee, called Nazareth, to a virgin," that is,
from the Most High to the most humble, from the
Lord to the hand-maid, from the Creator to the
creature. How great a condescension on the part of
God ! How great an exaltation for the Virgin ! Come
hither in haste, all ye mothers ; come hither, ye daughters ;
come hither all ye who after Eve and on account of
Eve have been condemned to bring forth in sorrow.
Draw near to this virginal sanctuary. Enter, if you
can, your Sister's modest chamber. Behold, she has
received a message from the Lord ! Behold, an archangel is conversing with Mary ! Put your ear to the
door and try to catch what he says to her. Perhaps
you shall hear something that may be a source of
consolation.

Rejoice, O father Adam, but thou still more, O
mother Eve ! Rejoice and be glad, both of you, who
have been the destroyers of us all, as you are the
parents of us all and, what added to the misery, you
were our destroyers even before you became our
parents. Let both of you, I say, find consolation in
this Daughter, so singularly endowed and so highly
privileged, but thou, especially, from whom the evil
originally took its rise and whose reproach has descended upon all women. For behold the time is at

hand when that curse shall be taken away, and when the woman shall no longer deserve to be complained of by her husband, who, whilst foolishly attempting to exonerate himself, did not shrink from the cruelty of accusing his wife, saying, " The woman whom Thou gavest me to be my companion, gave me of the tree and I did eat." Run, then, O Eve, run to Mary. Take refuge, O mother, with thy Daughter. Let the Daughter answer for the mother, let her take away her mother's reproach ; let her make satisfaction to the man for the woman's transgression. For if the man originally fell by the woman, it is also by the woman that he is now lifted up. What is that thou didst say, O Adam ? " The woman whom Thou gavest me to be my companion, gave me of the tree and I did eat." These are "words of malice," and, instead of excusing, rather increase thy fault. Nevertheless, Wisdom gained the victory over malice, because the reason for pardoning which God tried to obtain from thee, by His questioning, but could not, He has discovered in the treasury of His own inexhaustible mercy. Another woman is now given thee in place of the first, a prudent and humble Eve instead of the proud and foolish one, an Eve who shall offer thee, not the tree of death but the Bread of Life, and who shall yield thee, not the poisoned fruit of bitterness but the delicious fruit of immortality. Change thou, therefore, the wicked words of self-excuse into the voice of praise and thanksgiving, and say to the Lord, " The woman whom Thou gavest me, gave me of the tree of life and I did eat ; and it has become in my mouth sweeter than honey, because in it Thou hast given me life." Behold here the purpose for which the Angel was sent from

God to the Virgin. O Virgin, worthy of all admiration, deserving of all honour! O most wonderful of women and venerable over all, who hast repaired the ruin which our parents wrought and recovered life for their posterity!

"The Angel Gabriel," says the Evangelist, "was sent to a virgin," that is, to one who was a virgin in body, a virgin in mind, a virgin who had sealed her virginity by vow, such a virgin as the Apostle describes as "holy both in body and in spirit"; to a virgin not newly discovered nor discovered by chance, but chosen from eternity, foreknown and prepared for Himself by the Most High, guarded by angels, exhibited by the patriarchs under types and figures, announced from afar by the prophets. "Search the Scriptures" and verify what I say. Or do you wish that I should adduce here some of the relevant testimonies? Well, I shall present you with a few out of many. Of whom, then, if not of the Virgin, does the Lord appear to have spoken when He said to the serpent, "I will put enmities between thee and the woman"? But if you are not yet convinced that He was alluding to Mary, attend to what follows, "She * shall crush thy head." For whom but Mary was that victory reserved? She undoubtedly crushed the serpent's venemous head by bringing to naught every attempt of the wicked one to seduce her with his suggestions of pleasure and pride.

Again, whom else but Mary was Solomon seeking when he asked, "Who shall find a valiant woman?" For, being a man of great wisdom, he knew how

---

* So it is read in the Vulgate and some other Versions ; but according to the Greek and the Hebrew it is the woman's Seed that shall crush the serpent's head —(Translator).

fragile was the female sex, how weak in body and inconstant in mind.* But he knew also from the Scriptures the promise made by God—and it seemed to him only natural—that he who had conquered by a woman should be conquered by a woman. And hence he cried out in an excess of admiration, "Who shall find a valiant woman?" That is to say, "If the salvation of us all, and the recovery of our innocence, and our victory over Satan, thus depend upon a woman, it is absolutely essential to find a valiant woman, who shall be capable of accomplishing so difficult a task. But who shall find such a valiant woman?" However, lest anyone should suppose that he says this in despair, he adds, speaking as a prophet, "Far and far from the uttermost bounds is the price of her." That is, not vile, not little, not ordinary, not even of the earth, is the worth of this valiant woman, but it must be sought in heaven, and not in the heaven which is nearest to us, but "its going out is from the highest heaven." In the next place consider that bush which Moses once beheld giving forth flames of fire without being burnt. Was not this a type of Mary bringing forth her Infant without feeling the pangs of child-birth? † And the dry rod of Aaron that "bloomed blossoms," do you not recognise here a figure of her who conceived although she knew not man? Thus the great miracle of the flowering rod contained a mystery still greater; and it is of this

* Compare Virgil: "Varium et mutabile semper femina."—
Æn. iv. 569-570.
† It is also understood as symbolising her perpetual virginity. Hence the Church sings, "Rubum quem viderat Moyses incombustum conservatam agnovimus tuam laudabilem virginitatem" (Third Antiphon for Vespers of the Feast of Circumcision) —(Translator).

the Prophet Isaias speaks where he says, " There shall
come forth a rod out of the root of Jesse, and a flower
shall rise up out of his root," signifying by the rod
the Virgin, and by the flower of the rod the Virgin's
Offspring.

It may appear to you that what has just been said,
namely, that Christ is represented by the flower, is
opposed to my previous interpretation of this passage,
according to which it is not the flower of the rod
that symbolises Him, but the fruit of the flower. You
must know, however, that in the same rod of Aaron
(which not only " bloomed blossoms" but also put
forth leaves and fruit) we have types of Christ in the
leaves and fruit as well as in the blossom. You must
know also that in Moses He is designated by neither
the fruit nor the flower of the rod, but by the rod
itself, with which the Lawgiver on one occasion struck
the water and divided it for the people to cross,* and
on another the rock, causing a fountain to spring
forth for the refreshment of the thirsty.   For there
is nothing incongruous in different things representing
Christ under different aspects.   Thus the rod reminds
us of His power ; the flower of the good odour of His
fame ; the fruit of His sweetness ; the leaves of His
ever-watchful providence, whereby He never refuses to
protect under the shadow of His wings all that flee
to Him, either from the heat of carnal desires, or from
the fury of the impious who afflict them.   Oh, how
sweet and desirable it is to be sheltered under the

* Cf. Exodus xiv. 21. It is not said that Moses struck the
water with his rod, but that " when Moses stretched his hand
over the sea, the Lord took it away by a strong and burning
wind blowing all the night, and turned it into dry ground :
and the water was divided "—(Translator).

wings of Jesus, where the persecuted find a safe
asylum and the weary rest and refreshment! " Have
mercy on me," Lord Jesus, " have mercy on me, for
my soul trusteth in Thee, and in the shadow of Thy
wings will I hope until iniquity pass away." Yet, in
the testimony quoted from Isaias, the flower must be
understood to symbolise the Son and the rod as relating to the Mother ; because just as the rod " bloomed
blossoms " without seed, so did the Virgin conceive
without man's co-operation ; and as the putting forth
of the flower did not destroy the freshness of the rod,
so neither did her sacred child-birth injure Mary's
virginity.

Let me now bring forward a few more Scriptural
testimonies relating to the Virgin Mother and her
Divine Son.   The fleece of Gideon, which he had shorn
from the flesh of the sheep without wounding that
flesh, and which, when laid on the floor, was at one
time found all wet with dew, though the place about
it was dry, at another as dry as the ground was before,
whilst now the ground was drenched—what does this fleece
signify, if not the flesh assumed from the flesh of the
Virgin, without prejudice to her virginity ? * For it was
upon her that heaven rained down its mystical dew
what time the Fulness of the Divinity poured Itself
" corporally" into her bosom, so that of her plenitude
we might all receive, who without her should be
nothing better than dry earth.   To this twofold miracle,
granted to Gideon's prayer, the Psalmist seems to refer

* This interpretation is adopted by the Church in the second
antiphon of Vespers of the Feast of Circumcision : " quando
natus es ineffabiliter ex virgine, tunc impletae sunt Scripturae :
sicut pluvia in vellus descendisti ut salvum faceres genus
humanum "—(Translator).

very beautifully, when he says, speaking of Christ, " He shall come down like rain upon the fleece, and as showers gently falling upon the earth," alluding in the first part of the verse to the instance in which the fleece was found wet and the floor dry, in the second part to that in which the contrary was the case. For that " voluntary rain " which God hath " set aside for His inheritance " descended first into the Virgin's womb, most gently and softly, without the noise and bustle characteristic of human operations. Afterwards it was spread through the world by the mouths of preachers, no longer falling as dew upon the fleece, but descending as showers upon the earth, amidst the clamour of tongues and the tumult of miracles. For those spiritual clouds * who carried this rain remembered the command given them when they received their mission, " That which I tell you in the dark, speak ye in the light ; and that which you hear in the ear, preach ye upon the house-tops." And so indeed they acted, because, as the Prophet had predicted of them, " Their sound hath gone forth into all the earth, and their words unto the ends of the world."

Let us next hear Jeremias announcing a new wonder to the ancients, whilst he longs for with ardour and faithfully promises the coming of Him Whom he was not able to point out as actually present. " The Lord," he says, " hath created a new thing upon the earth ; a woman shall compass a man." Now, who is this woman ? And who is this man ? If he be a

---

* " Qui sunt isti, qui ut nubes volant ? " (Is. lx. 8), used as Responsary for fourth lesson, second nocturn of the common of Apostles (Cistercian Breviary)—(Translator).

man, how can he be compassed by a woman? And
if he be compassed by a woman, how is he a man?
To speak more plainly, how is it possible for him to
be a man and at the same time to be enclosed within
his mother's womb? For this is what the Prophet
means when he says a woman shall encompass a man.
Those, as you know, are called men, who, after passing
through the periods of infancy, boyhood, adolescence,
and early manhood, have attained to that which is
followed by old age. How then can one who is so
advanced be compassed by a woman? Had the
Prophet merely proclaimed that a woman should
compass an infant, or that a woman should compass
a little one, he would have predicted nothing new,
nothing marvellous. Such, however, was not his
announcement, but that " a woman shall compass a
man." It is therefore incumbent on us to inquire
into the meaning of this " new thing " which the
Lord "hath created upon the earth," that a woman
should compass a man, and that a man should be
so contracted as to be confined within the womb
of a woman. What manner of miracle is this? " Can
a man enter a second time into his mother's womb,"
asked Nicodemus, " and be born again? "

Let us turn to the conception and child-birth of the
Virgin. Perhaps amongst the many wonders and prodigies which shall certainly be found there by diligent
inquiry, I may also discover that "new thing" whereof the
Prophet Jeremias speaks. There, beyond doubt, I behold
eternity shortened, Immensity contracted, Sublimity
levelled down, Profundity made shallow. I contemplate there Light without splendour, the Word without
speech, Water Which is thirsty, and Bread That feels

hunger. There, too, if thou art attentive, thou mayest notice Omnipotence being ruled, Omniscience being instructed, Virtue supported, God feeding at the breast whilst He nourishes the angels, God wailing with grief whilst consoling the wretched. Thou shalt there, if thou observest, see Joy a prey to sadness, Confidence fearful, Health in suffering, Life enduring death, Strength rendered feeble. Aye, and what is not less astonishing, thou mayest there discover sadness giving joy, fear producing confidence, suffering a source of health, death communicating life, weakness imparting strength. And surely there is none who does not already recognise here that other miracle for which I have been seeking. Is it not easy to discern amongst the prodigies just enumerated, that of the woman compassing the man, when we behold Mary enclosing in her womb " Jesus, a Man approved of God "? For I call Jesus a man not only when He was described as a " Man Who was a Prophet, mighty in word and work before God and all the people," but also, when His Mother, the Mother of God, either bore Him in her womb, or as a tender Infant fondly nursed Him on her lap. Therefore, even whilst He was yet unborn, Jesus was a man, a man not in age but in wisdom, not in bodily strength but in vigour of mind, not in the development of His physical members, but in the maturity of His mental powers. For Jesus was not less wise, or rather I should say, was not less Wisdom, whilst still in the womb than after His birth, when He was a little one than when He was full-grown. Whether, then, we consider Him as the Babe unborn, or as the Infant wailing in the crib, or as the grown-up Boy, questioning the doctors in the temple, or as the Man of mature age teaching the multitude, He was always and equally full of the Holy Ghost. There was not a moment at any period of His life when that fulness which He received at His conception was either increased by anything or by anything diminished; because from the beginning He was perfect, from the beginning I say, He was full " of the Spirit of wisdom and of understanding, of the Spirit of counsel and of fortitude, of the Spirit of knowledge and of piety, of the Spirit of the fear of the Lord."

Do not think there is anything inconsistent in what I have been saying with that which is written in St. Luke, " And Jesus advanced in wisdom and age, and grace with God and man." For what is here said of His growth in wisdom and grace must be understood, not of these qualities in themselves, but of their outward manifestation : not in the sense that anything was added to Him which He had not before, but only that there was an appearance of such an addition whenever He willed it to be so.* Thou, O man, when thou progressest, dost not go forward when thou wilt nor as far as thou wilt. Although thou perceivest it not, thy progress is regulated and thy life ordered by Another. But Jesus, Who disposes thy life, had the disposition of His own life also ; and to whom He willed, and when He willed, He showed Himself wise or more wise, or most wise, although in Himself He was never anything but most wise. Similarly, though He was always full of all grace, both that which must be exhibited to the eyes of God and that which is

---

* St. Thomas answers the question : Did Christ make progress in knowledge ? in almost the same words. Cf. *Sum. Theol.*, III. q. xii. a. 2. In Sermon LVI. on the Canticle St. Bernard teaches that there was real progress in Christ's *experimental* knowledge —(Translator).

owing to men, He nevertheless made it manifest, at
His pleasure, in greater or lesser degree, according to
what He knew was consonant with the merits or expedient for the salvation of the beholders. It is evident,
then, that with respect to the faculties and endow-
ments of His Soul, Jesus was always a man, although
He did not always appear with a fully developed
body. For why should I doubt that He was a man
in the womb when I have no doubt that He was God
in the womb ? Surely, it is not so great a thing to
be a man as to be God? But see if the Prophet
Isaias, who has already told us the meaning of the
fresh flowers on Aaron's rod, does not also explain
for us most clearly this strange prodigy announced by
Jeremias. " Behold," he says, " a virgin shall conceive and bear a Son." Here you have the woman
that is to compass a man, namely, the Virgin. And
as to the man, do you desire to know who he is ?
" And his name shall be called Emmanuel, that is,
God-with-us." Therefore, the woman compassing the
man is the Virgin Mother conceiving God. Observe here
how beautifully and how harmoniously the miraculous
deeds * and the mystical words of holy men combine
and fit together. Remark also how stupendous must
have been this one miracle wrought in relation to the
Virgin and within the Virgin, since it was heralded by so
many wonders, and promised by so many oracles. All
the prophets had the same Spirit, and all, however much
they differed from each other in other respects, foresaw
and predicted in the same Spirit the same great truth,
at various times, in various manners, and under various

* He alludes to what he has related from the histories of
Moses, Aaron, and Gideon —(Translator).

figures. What was revealed to Moses in the bush and the fire, to Aaron in the rod and the flower, to Gideon in the fleece and the dew : the same was clearly announced by Solomon in the valiant woman and her price, more clearly still by Jeremias in the woman and the man she was to compass, and most clearly by Isaias, who explained it of God and the Virgin, and was finally exhibited to view when Gabriel saluted Mary. For the Virgin mentioned by the Prophet is the same of whom the Evangelist writes, " The Angel Gabriel was sent from God to a virgin espoused to a man whose name was Joseph of the house of David, and the Virgin's name was Mary."

" To a virgin espoused." Wherefore * was she espoused ? Being, I say, a virgin elect, and, as has been shown, destined to conceive as a virgin, and to bring forth as a virgin, it may seem strange that she should have contracted an engagement which was never to be consummated in marriage. No one surely will be foolish enough to say that this was due to chance. That is certainly not the result of chance which appears to be commended by a rational purpose, aye, by a most useful and necessary purpose, a purpose worthy of the counsels of divine wisdom. I will now say what I think on this subject, or rather I will offer the explanation which has occurred to the fathers before me. The reason, then, of Mary's espousals was the same as that for which the Apostle Thomas was permitted to doubt. It was a Jewish custom that from the day of the betrothal to that appointed for the nuptials, the affianced should be placed under

* From this paragraph are taken the lessons of the third nocturn for the Feast of St. Joseph, March 19th —(Translator).

the care of her intended husband, who would watch
over the virtue of his future wife with a diligence
proportionate to his regard for his own honour. Therefore, just as Thomas, by first doubting the truth and
then proving it by the testimony of his touch, was
made a most firm confessor of the Lord's resurrection,
so also Joseph, by espousing to himself Mary and by
closely observing her conduct during the time of engagement, became a most trustworthy witness of her
virtue. There is thus a beautiful resemblance between
the espousals of the Virgin and the Apostle's doubt.
Each of the two was in itself well calculated to entangle us in the meshes of a similar net of error ; that
is to say, Thomas's doubt might have caused us to
suspect his faith, and Mary's betrothal her virtue.
But in both cases, the matter was arranged with such
prudence and piety that what should naturally have
aroused suspicion has been made the very means of
confirming our faith. For, with respect to the resurrection of the Son, I, because I am weak, should more
readily believe Thomas, who doubted, and could only
be convinced by the evidence of his senses, than Cephas,
who assented to the truth as soon as it was announced
to him. And as to the Mother's integrity, I should
find it easier to accept the testimony of Joseph, her
guardian and associate, than that of the Virgin defend-
ing herself by the sole witness of her own conscience.
Who, I ask, seeing her with child before marriage,
would not rather declare her a sinner than a virgin ?
Now it would have been altogether unbecoming that
anything such should be said of the Mother of God.
It was more tolerable and more proper that, for a
time, Christ should be considered to have been born

in wedlock in the ordinary way, than born of a sinner.*

Perhaps it will be said, could not God have given some manifest sign which would at once safeguard the virgin birth and demonstrate the mother's innocence ? Undoubtedly. But that which men would know could not be kept secret from the demon. Now it was necessary to conceal for a while from " the prince of this world " the grand design of the divine wisdom. Not that God, if He willed to accomplish His purpose openly, could have any fear of being prevented by Satan. But because, as He " hath done all things whatsoever He would," not only with might, but also with wisdom, and as He is wont in His other works to attend to the fittingness of things and of seasons, out of regard for order and beauty, so too, in this most magnificent of His works, the work, namely, of our redemption, He willed to display His prudence as well as His power. And although, had He so wished, He could have wrought our salvation in a different manner, nevertheless He preferred to reconcile us to Himself in the way and order in which He knew we had lapsed. Hence, as the devil first seduced the woman and then by the woman conquered the man : so he was to be in turn first deceived by another woman, viz., the

* Compare the following from St. Ambrose : " Cur autem non antequam desponsaretur (Maria) impleta est ? Fortasse ne diceretur quod conceperat ex adulterio. Et bene utrumque posuit Scriptura, ut et desponsata est et virgo. Virgo, ut expers virilis consortii videretur. Desponsata, ne temeratae virginitatis aduraretur infamia, cui gravis alvus corruptelae videretur insigne praeferre. Maluit autem Dominus aliquos de sui ortu quam de matris pudore dubitare. Sciebat enim teneram esse virginis verecundiam et lubricam famam pudoris : nec putavit ortus sui fidem matris injuriis astruendam " (*In Lucam*, l. 11) — (Translator).

Virgin Mary, and next openly vanquished by another
man, that is, by Christ. Thus, whilst the wisdom of
piety overreached the cunning of malice, and the
virtue of Christ overcame the power of the wicked
one, God would be revealed as at once more mighty
and more prudent than Satan. So it became incarnate
Wisdom to conquer spiritual malice, in order that He
might not only " reach from end to end powerfully "
but at the same time " dispose all things sweetly."
Now, He had already in truth "reached from end to
end," that is, from the height of heaven to the depth of
the abyss ; and hence the Psalmist says, " If I ascend
into heaven, Thou art there ; if I descend into hell, Thou
art present." And to both these extremes He had
" reached mightily," since from heaven He had banished
the proud, and in hell despoiled the greedy. It was
fitting, therefore, that He should likewise " dispose all
things sweetly," in heaven and on earth, that, after
driving forth the disturber from paradise, He should
establish the rest in peace, and descending hither to
overthrow the envious one, should first give us the
very necessary example of His meekness and humility.
Thus should it come to pass by a marvellous arrange-
ment of divine wisdom that He would appear sweet
to His friends and mighty to His enemies. The example of His humility I have said, was necessary to
us, for where would be the profit of God's triumph
over Satan if we continued proud ? There was good
reason, therefore, why Mary should be espoused to
Joseph, since in this way that which was so holy was
kept hidden from the dogs, the virtue of the Mother
had the witness of her spouse, and at the same time a
defence was provided for the Virgin's modesty and

fair fame.* Could anything be more prudent or more worthy of divine providence ? By this single device three objects were attained : the heavenly secret was revealed to Joseph so that he might give testimony of it, it was concealed from the enemy, whilst the Mother's good name was preserved intact. Without such knowledge how could the just Joseph have spared her whom he must have thought a sinner ? It is written, however, " Whereupon Joseph, her husband, being a just man, and not willing publicly to expose her, was minded to put her away privately." Well does the Evangelist say that, " being a just man," he was unwilling to expose her ; because, as he would not have been just had he spared one whom he knew to be guilty, so neither would he have been just if he condemned one of whose innocence he had had proof. Therefore, "being a just man and not willing publicly to expose her, he was minded to put her away privately."

But why was he " minded to put her away," if conscious of her innocence ? Here again I will offer an explanation not excogitated by myself, but derived from the fathers. Joseph wished to put away his spouse for the same reason on account of which Peter begged of the Lord to leave him, exclaiming, " Depart from me, O Lord, for I am a sinful man," and on account of which the Centurion prayed that He would

---

* St. Jerome assigns the following reasons for Mary's espousals (*Comment. in Matth.* l. 1, c. i.), " Quare non de simplici virgine concipitur (Christus) ? Primum, ut per generationem Joseph, origo Mariae monstraretur ; secundo, ne lapidaretur a Judaeis ut adultera ; tertio, ut in Aegyptum fugiens haberet solatium. Martyr Ignatius etiam quartam addidit causam cur a sponsata conceptus sit : ut partus, inquiens, ejus celaretur a diabolo, dum putat eum non de virgine sed de uxore generatum." See also St. Thomas, *Sum. Theol.*, III. q. xxix. a. 1.—(Translator).

not enter his house, saying, " Lord, I am not worthy
that Thou shouldst enter under my roof." Thus
Joseph also, considering himself unworthy and a
sinner, said to himself that it was not befitting for a
man like him to live any longer in such intimate
relations with one so great and exalted, whose sublime
dignity inspired him with awe. He trembled on beholding by the clearest indications that she bore in her
bosom the Divinity incarnate; and as he could not
fathom the mystery, he " was minded to put her
away." Peter was frightened at the omnipotence of
God; the Centurion feared the Majesty of His presence. In the same way this prodigy, so great and
so unparalleled, this mystery, so dark and profound,
alarmed Joseph, who was but a man, and hence he
was " minded to put her away." How can you wonder
that Joseph deemed himself unworthy of the Virgin
Mother's society when you hear from St. Elizabeth
that she could not endure the presence of Mary except
with fear and awe? For thus she exclaims : " Whence
is this to me that the Mother of my Lord should come
to me ? " Here, then, is the reason for which Joseph
" was minded to put her away." * But wherefore
secretly and not rather publicly? It was doubtless
to prevent any questions being asked with regard to
the separation, and to avoid the necessity of revealing
the cause. For what answer could the holy man have
given to that stiff-necked people, to that people " not
believing and contradicting " ? Were he to tell them
all he knew and the proofs he had of her innocence,

* Amongst the supporters of this opinion are Origen, St.
Basil, and St. Jerome : also St. Bridget (*Revel.* l. vii., c. **xxx.**),
who claims that its truth was supernaturally made known to
her. (Cf. A Lapide, *Comment. in Matth.* c. i.) —(Translator).

would they not, those cruel and incredulous Jews,
instead of being persuaded, rather have mocked at
him and stoned her? They who, later on, despised and
rejected Truth crying out in the temple, how could
they have believed Truth when hidden in the womb?
What would they have done to Him whilst yet unborn,
on Whom afterwards, when glorified by miracles, they
did not hesitate to lay sacrilegious hands? With
reason therefore was the just man "minded to put
her away privately," lest otherwise he should be compelled either to lie or to defame the innocent.

Should anyone, however, prefer a different explanation, and believe that Joseph doubted from human
reasons, that, "being a just man," he was unwilling
to live with one whom he suspected, yet, being also
merciful, he would not expose her, and so "was minded
to put her away privately": I answer briefly that even
thus Joseph's doubting was without blame, seeing that
he was deemed worthy of being enlightened by a
heavenly oracle. For, as the Evangelist tells us, "while
he thought on these things (that is, how he might put
her away privately) behold the angel of the Lord
appeared to him in his sleep, saying: Joseph, son of
David, fear not to take unto thee Mary thy wife, for
that which is conceived in her is of the Holy Ghost."
Such, therefore, are the reasons why Mary was espoused
to Joseph, or rather, as the Evangelist expresses it,
" to a man whose name was Joseph." He calls Joseph
a man (*vir*) not because he was Mary's husband, but
to indicate that he was endowed with virtue (*homo
virtutis*). Or, since he is called her husband by another
Evangelist, it may be said that, as he necessarily
seemed to stand in that relation to her, he was justly

entitled to the name. It was therefore right to speak of him as if he really were what people could not help supposing him ; just as he also merited, not indeed to be, but to be called and reputed the father of the Saviour. So we read in St. Luke, " And Jesus Himself was beginning about the age of thirty years : being (as it was supposed) the Son of Joseph." Consequently, he was in reality no more the husband of the Mother than he was the father of the Child, although, as I have said, he was called and reputed both for a time, by a special and necessary dispensation.*

What † and how great was the dignity of Joseph you may learn from this title, wherewith, although it was purely official, he merited to be honoured by God, so

* Similarly St. Jerome (*Comment. in Matth.* i. 16), " Cum virum audieris suspicio tibi non subeat nuptiarum, sed recordare consuetudinis scripturarum, quod sponsi viri et sponsae uxores vocantur." But it is evident that what both doctors deny is that St. Joseph was Mary's husband in a sense which would be incompatible with her virginity : that the marriage between them was not only " ratum," but also " consummatum." Hence St. Thomas writes (*Sum. Theol.*, III. q. xxix. a. 2), " Dicendum quod matrimonium dicitur verum ex hoc quod suam perfectionem attingit. Duplex est autem rei perfectio, prima et secunda. Prima quidem rei perfectio consistit in ipsa forma ex qua speciem sortitur. Secunda vero perfectio consistit in operatione rei per quam res aliqualiter suum finem attingit. Forma autem matrimonii consistit in quadam indivisibili conjunctione animorum, per quam unus conjugum indivisibiliter alteri fidem servare tenetur. Finis autem matrimonii est proles generanda et educanda : ad quorum primum pervenitur per actum conjugalem, ad secundum per alia opera viri et uxoris, quibus sibi invicem obsequuntur ad prolem nutriendam.

" Sic igitur dicendum est quod quantum ad primam perfectionem, omnino fuit verum matrimonium Virginis Matris Dei et Joseph . ; . quantum vero ad secundam perfectionem quae est per actum matrimonii . . . non fuit illud matrimonium consummatum." See also A Lapide, *Comment. in Matth.* i. 18. —(Translator).

† The lessons of the second nocturn for the Feast of St. Joseph are taken from this paragraph —(Translator).

that he was called and considered the father of God.
It may also be conjectured from his own proper name,
which undoubtedly signifies " increase." Remember at
the same time that illustrious Patriarch who was sold
of yore into Egypt, and be assured that Mary's spouse
has inherited not only his name, but also his chastity,
his grace, and his innocence. The elder Joseph, in his
being sold into Egypt through the envy of his brethren,
typified the betrayal of Christ by His Apostle ; whilst
the younger, to escape from the envy of King Herod,
fled into Egypt by night with the Saviour. The former,
true to his allegiance, respected his master's honour in
his mistress ; the latter recognising in his spouse the
Virgin Mother of his Lord, became the witness and
the guardian of her integrity. The former was gifted
with the power of understanding prophetic dreams ; the
latter was privileged to become the confidant of God's
mysterious designs and a co-operator in their accomplishment. The one preserved the corn, not for himself
but for the people ; the other was chosen to preserve,
both for himself and for all the world, " the Living
Bread That came down from heaven." There can be
no manner of doubt that this Joseph, to whom was
espoused the Saviour's Mother, was singularly good
and faithful. He was, I say, the good and faithful
servant, whom the Lord appointed to be the consolation of His Mother, the support of His Humanity,
and His one most faithful coadjutor on earth in the
execution of His mighty purpose. To this must be
added that he is declared to have been of the house
of David. Truly this Joseph was descended from
David, truly he came of a royal stock, yet though noble
by his ancestry, he was nobler still by his virtues and

character. He was indeed the son of David, and well worthy to have David for his father. He was, I say, the son of David, and that, not only according to the flesh, but also by his faith, by his sanctity, and by his devotion. Him, like another David, the Lord found to be a man according to His own Heart, and one to whom He might safely entrust the most hidden and the most holy secret of His mind. To him, therefore, as to his father David, He " made known the uncertain and hidden things of His wisdom " ; and He admitted him to the knowledge of the mystery " which none of the princes of this world knew." Yea, and Him Whom " many kings and prophets desired to see and did not see," desired to hear and did not hear, Him it was granted to Joseph not only to see and to hear, but even to carry in his arms, to lead by the hand, to embrace, to kiss, to support, and to protect. But we must believe that Mary as well as Joseph was descended from David. For unless she also belonged to the house of David she could not have been espoused to one of that royal stock.* Therefore both Mary and Joseph were of David's line, and in Mary was fulfilled the promise which the Lord gave under oath to David, whilst it was Joseph's office to be cognisant of that fulfilment and to bear witness to the same.

At the end of the verse occur these words, " And the Virgin's name was Mary." Let me say something

* " The intelligent reader may ask, why does the Evangelist give us the genealogy of Joseph, since he is not the father of Christ ? To this I answer, in the first place, that it is not in accordance with Scriptural usage to make mention of women in genealogies ; and secondly, that Joseph and Mary belonged to the same tribe : hence the law obliged him to marry her as his cousin, and as belonging to the same family, they were enrolled together at Bethlehem " (St. Jerome, *Comment. in Matth.*, l. i.) — (Translator).

concerning this name also, which is interpreted to mean "Star of the sea," and admirably suits the Virgin Mother.* There is indeed a wonderful appropriateness in this comparison of her to a star, because as a star sends out its ray without detriment to itself, so did the Virgin bring forth her Child without injury to her integrity. And as the ray emitted does not diminish the brightness of the star, so neither did the Child born of her tarnish the beauty of Mary's virginity. She is therefore that glorious star, which, according to prophecy, arose out of Jacob, whose ray illumines the entire earth, whose splendour shines out conspicuously in heaven and reaches even unto hell; a star which, enlightening the universe, and communicating warmth rather to souls than to bodies, fosters virtue and extinguishes vice. She, I say, is that resplendent and radiant star, placed as a necessary beacon above life's "great and spacious sea," glittering with merits, luminous with examples for our imitation. Oh, whosoever thou art that perceivest thyself during this mortal existence to be rather floating in the treacherous waters, at the mercy of the winds and the waves, than walking secure on the stable earth, turn not away thine eyes from the splendour of this guiding star, unless thou wishest to be submerged by the tempest! When the storms of temptation burst upon

* There are various other interpretations of this name. "Mary signifies 'the sea,' because by her merits and intercession she washes us from our sins"—St. Antoninus. "Mary means 'enlightener,' because she brought forth the Light of the world. In the Syriac tongue, Mary signifies 'Lady'"—St. Isidore. St. Thomas follows St. Bernard: "Mary means 'star of the sea,' because just as the star of the sea guides the navigators to port, so does Mary guide Christians to glory"—Opusc. 8, super Ave Maria —(Translator).

thee, when thou seest thyself driven upon the rocks of tribulation, look up at the star, call upon Mary. When buffeted by the billows of pride, or ambition, or hatred, or jealousy, look up at the star, call upon Mary. Should anger, or avarice, or carnal desires violently assail the little vessel of thy soul, look up at the star, call upon Mary. If troubled on account of the heinousness of thy sins, confounded at the filthy state of thy conscience, and terrified at the thought of the awful judgment to come, thou art beginning to sink into the bottomless gulf of sadness and to be absorbed in the abyss of despair, oh, then think of Mary! In dangers, in doubts, in difficulties, think of Mary, call upon Mary. Let not her name depart from thy lips, never suffer it to leave thy heart. And that thou mayest more surely obtain the assistance of her prayer, neglect not to walk in her footsteps. With her for guide, thou shalt never go astray; whilst invoking her, thou shalt never lose heart; so long as she is in thy mind, thou art safe from deception; whilst she holds thy hand, thou canst not fall; under her protection, thou hast nothing to fear; if she walks before thee, thou shalt not grow weary; if she shows thee favour, thou shalt reach the goal. And thus thou shalt experience in thyself the truth of what is written, " And the Virgin's name was Mary."* But here we must pause for a

* Compare the following eloquent passage from Cardinal Newman :—

" O my dear children, young men and young women, what need have you of the intercession of the Virgin Mother, of her help, of her pattern! What shall bring you forward in the narrow way, if you live in the world, but the thought and patronage of Mary? What shall seal your senses, what shall tranquillise your heart, when sights and sounds of danger are around you, but the thought of Mary? What shall give you patience and endurance when you are wearied out with the

brief space, in order that we may contemplate a while
the splendour of so grand a luminary. For, to use
the words of the Apostle Peter, " it is good for us to
be here " ; and I prefer the delight of gazing in silence
upon that which no laboured eloquence can sufficiently
describe. Besides, the devout contemplation of this
resplendent star shall enable me to address myself with
increased fervour to the other discussions which are to
follow.

length of the conflict with evil, with the unceasing necessity
of precautions, with the irksomeness of observing them, with
the tediousness of their repetition, with the strain upon your
mind, with your forlorn and cheerless condition, but a loving
communion with her ? She will comfort you in your discour-
agements, solace you in your fatigue, raise you up after your
falls, reward you for your successes. She will show you her
Son, your God and your all. When your spirit within you is
excited, or relaxed, or depressed, when it loses its balance,
when it is restless and wayward, when it is sick of what it has
and hankers after what it has not, when your eye is solicited
with evil, and your mortal frame trembles under the shadow
of the Tempter, what will bring you to yourselves, to peace
and to health, but the cool breath of the Immaculate and the
fragrance of the Rose of Sharon ? "—*Discourses to Mixed Congregations*, pp. 400-401.

III

THIRD SERMON ON THE GLORIES OF THE VIRGIN MOTHER

"And the Angel, being come in, said unto her : Hail, full of grace, the Lord is with thee ; Blessed art thou among women.

" Who having heard, was troubled at his saying, and thought with herself what manner of salutation this should be.

" And so the Angel said to her : Fear not, Mary, for thou hast found grace with God.

" Behold thou shalt conceive in thy womb, and shalt bring forth a son : and thou shalt call His name Jesus.

" He shall be great, and shall be called the son of the Most High, and the Lord God shall give unto Him the throne of David, His Father ; and He shall reign in the house of Jacob for ever "—Luke i. 28–32.

I am always glad to borrow the language of the saints, whenever I find that it suits my purpose, in the hope that at least the beauty of the expression may commend to my readers or hearers the thoughts which I desire to communicate. Hence I begin this discourse by saying with the Prophet, " Woe is me," not indeed because, like Isaias, " I have held my peace," but because I have spoken, " for I am a man of unclean lips." Alas for me ! What words of vanity, of deceit, and of shame do I not remember to have vomited forth from this most filthy mouth of mine with which I now presume to speak the language of heaven ! I am very much afraid that I shall soon hear addressed to me these words of reproof, " Why dost thou declare My justices and take My covenant in thy mouth ? " Would to God that I were presented, not as the Prophet, with a single live coal from the heavenly altar, but with an immense volume of flame, which might suffice to burn out completely the thick and inveterate rust

40

of sin that covers my restless tongue ! So should I, perhaps, be deemed worthy to comment in my own poor discourse on the words of modesty and sweetness interchanged between the Angel and the Virgin. Well. The Evangelist proceeds, " And the Angel being come in, said unto her—that is, unto Mary—Hail, full of grace, the Lord is with thee." In whither did Gabriel come ? In my opinion, it was into the privacy of her modest bed-chamber, where, perhaps, having shut the door upon herself, she was praying to the Father in secret. For the angels are wont to draw nigh to us when we pray, and to rejoice at the prayer we make with pure hands raised up to heaven. It is a pleasure for them to offer to God, as an odour of sweetness, the holo- caust of our fervent devotion. And how pleasing in the sight of the Most High were the prayers of Mary, Gabriel indicated by the reverence with which he saluted her on entering. Nor was it difficult for the Angel to pass through the closed door into the Virgin's chamber, for in virtue of that subtlety which is a property of his spiritual nature, he could go whithersoever he pleased without experiencing any impediment, even from the obstruction of iron bars. Walls are not an obstacle to the flight of angelic spirits, nothing visible can hinder their movements, and there is no material substance, howsoever solid and dense it may be, which is not pervious and penetrable to them. We must not suppose, therefore, that Gabriel found the door of the Virgin's chamber ajar, since we know how anxious she was to shun the society of men and to avoid useless conversation, in order thus to preserve that silence so conducive to prayer, and to preclude the risk of tempta- tion. And so at that hour, Mary, as a most prudent virgin, had her door closed, not however against angels, but only to men.   Therefore, whilst beyond the reach of every man, she was easily accessible to Gabriel.

The Angel, accordingly, " being come in said to her : Hail, full of grace, the Lord is with thee." We read in the Acts of the Apostles that Stephen also was full of grace, and that the apostles were full of the Holy Ghost, but very differently from Mary.   For Stephen had not, like her, the fulness of the Divinity dwelling in him corporally, nor were the apostles, as was she, so full of the Holy Ghost as to conceive by Him.   And the Angel " said to her : Hail, full of grace." What wonder that she was full of grace since the Lord was with her ?   It is this that should rather surprise us, how He Who had sent the Angel to the Virgin was found by the same Angel to be with the Virgin.   Shall we then suppose that God came down more swiftly than Gabriel, and by His greater celerity outstripped His hurrying envoy in the descent from heaven to earth ?   But neither is there matter for wonder in this. For " while the King was at His repose," the Virgin's " spikenard sent forth the odour thereof," and the smoke of her aromatical spices ascended to the presence of His glory, and found favour in the sight of the Lord, the whole heavenly court crying out in admiration, " Who is she that goeth up by the desert as a pillar of smoke of aromatical spices, of myrrh, and frankincense, and of all the powders of the perfumer ? " The King immediately " went forth from His holy place " and " rejoiced as a giant to run the way "; and although " His going out is from the highest heaven," yet, flying with the wings of ardent affection, He outdistanced His messenger and was the first to reach the Virgin whom He loved, whom He had chosen, whose beauty He desired. It is this approach of His that the Church contemplates from afar when she exclaims with joy and exultation, " Behold He cometh, leaping upon the mountains, skipping over the hills."

Not without cause did the King desire the Virgin's beauty. For she had done that which her father, the Prophet David, had so long before recommended, saying to her in the Spirit, " Hearken, O daughter, and see, and incline thine ear : and forget thy people and thy father's house." (And then, when thou hast acted thus) " the King shall greatly desire thy beauty." The Virgin, therefore, hearkened and saw : not like some, who hear without heeding, and see without understanding ; because in her case hearing resulted in faith and sight in comprehension. She also inclined her ear to obedience and her heart to instruction ; and she forgot her people and her father's house. She forgot her people, for the increase of whom by marriage she had no solicitude ; and she forgot her father's house, since she had bound herself by vow not to leave it an heir. But whatever of temporal honour she could have had amongst her people, whatever of earthly riches from her father's house, she counted it all as dross that so she might gain Christ. And her desire was most fully accomplished, when, without prejudice to her vow of virginity, she obtained Christ for her Son. Rightly, therefore, is she pronounced full of grace who, endowed already with the grace of integrity, was now to add thereto the glory of fecundity.

" Hail, full of grace, the Lord is with thee." Notice how the Angel did not say " The Lord is *in* thee," but " the Lord is *with* thee." For God, Who by the

simplicity of His Essence is equally and entirely everywhere present, has nevertheless, by His influence and
operation, a presence in His rational creatures, which
He has not in others, and amongst the former, a
presence in the good different from that which He
has in the wicked. He is truly present in irrational
creatures, yet without being embraced by them. He
is in His rational creatures in such a manner that they
all have the power to embrace Him by knowledge, yet
only the good by love. Consequently, of the good
alone it can be said that He is so in them as to be
also with them, because of the harmony of their wills
with His. For whilst they so conform their wills to
the law of justice that it is not unworthy of God to
will what they will, there is established a concord
between His will and theirs, and thus they become
specially united with Him. But although this is the
case with every holy soul, it is particularly true of
Mary. So close was the union He contracted with her,
that He united to Himself not only her will, but even
her flesh ; and from His own Substance and the substance of the Virgin He fashioned one Christ, or rather
He became one Christ, Who, although neither wholly
from God nor wholly from Mary, yet belongs wholly
to God and wholly to Mary : nor are there two sons,
but the one same Christ is Son of both. The Angel
says, therefore, " Hail, full of grace, the Lord is with
thee." But, O Mary, the Lord with thee is not the
Son alone Whom thou hast clothed with thy flesh : He
is also the Holy Spirit, by Whom thou hast conceived,
and He is also the Father by Whom from eternity thy
Child is begotten. The Father, I say, is with thee,
Who has given His Son to be also thine. The Son is

with thee, Who in a marvellous way has entered thy
womb without detriment to thy virginity. The Holy
Ghost is with thee, Who, with the Father and the Son,
has prepared thy virginal body to be the dwelling of
the Word. Therefore " the Lord is with thee."

" Blessed art thou among women." To these words,
spoken both by the Angel and afterwards by Elizabeth,
I will join these others which the latter added, " And
blessed is the Fruit of thy womb." It is not because
thou, O Virgin, art blessed that therefore the Fruit of
thy womb is blessed, but on the contrary, therefore
art thou blessed, because He " hath prevented thee
with the blessings of sweetness." Truly blessed is the
Fruit of thy womb, for " in Him all the nations of the
earth shall be blessed," and it is of His fulness thou
also, His Mother, hast received with the rest, although
differently from the rest. And therefore art thou also
blessed, yet only among women: whereas He is blessed,
not alone amongst men, not alone amongst angels, but
absolutely, since He is the Same Who, according to
the Apostle, " is over all things, God blessed for ever."
We speak of blessed men, and blessed women, and
blessed bread, and blessed earth, and other creatures
also are said to be blessed : but uniquely blessed is the
Fruit of thy womb, " Who is over all things, God
blessed for ever."

Therefore, " blessed is the Fruit of thy womb,"
blessed in His odour, blessed in His taste, and blessed
in His beauty. Long ago the Patriarch Isaac inhaled
the perfume of this fragrant Fruit, when he cried out:
" Behold the smell of my Son is as the smell of a
plentiful field which the Lord hath blessed." Surely
He is blessed indeed, Who hath been blessed by the

Lord. And concerning the flavour of this Fruit, the Psalmist after enjoying it, broke forth into song and said, " Oh, taste and see that the Lord is sweet," and, " Oh, how great is the multitude of Thy sweetness, O Lord, which Thou hast hidden for them that fear Thee ! " And to the same the Apostle Peter thus refers, " If so be you have tasted that the Lord is sweet." Yea, the Fruit Himself, inviting us to Him, declares, " They that eat Me, shall yet hunger ; and they that drink Me shall yet thirst." He speaks thus, no doubt, on account of the sweetness of His taste, which, when once experienced, rather excites than appeases the appetite. That certainly is a noble Fruit, Which becomes the food and the drink of those who hunger and thirst after justice. I have spoken of the odour of this Fruit, and I have spoken of His taste : listen now to what I have to say about His beauty. For if the fruit of death was not only pleasing to the palate but also, as the Scripture bears witness, " delightful to behold," with how much greater eagerness should we not turn to contemplate the beauty of that life-giving Fruit " on Whom the angels desire to look " ? This beauty David beheld in the Spirit and longed to see in the flesh, since he said of it, " Out of Sion the loveliness of His beauty." And lest you should consider this but a slight commendation, recollect what is written in another psalm, " Thou art beautiful above the sons of men : grace is poured abroad on Thy lips : therefore hath God blessed Thee for ever."

" Blessed," then, O Mother, " is the Fruit of thy Womb," since God hath blessed Him for ever. And it is from the fulness of His blessing that thou thyself art blessed among women, because " an evil tree cannot

bring forth good fruit." " Blessed," I say, " art thou
among women," who alone of women hast escaped not
only that general curse pronounced against Eve in Paradise, " In sorrow shalt thou bring forth children," but this
other also, " Cursed be she that is barren in Israel " ;*
and hast instead obtained the singular blessing whereby
thou art made a mother without the penalty to bring
forth in pain. O cruel necessity and heavy yoke upon
all the hapless daughters of Eve! If they become
mothers they shall suffer anguish, and if they remain
sterile they shall be accurst. The pain debars them
from motherhood, the malediction from sterility. What
wilt thou do, O prudent Virgin, who hast heard and
read of this? Affliction awaits thee, if thou bringest
forth ; if thou remainest barren, the curse. Which,
then, wilt thou choose, O prudent Virgin? " I am
straitened," she seems to say, " on every side. Yet it
it is better for me to incur the malediction by remaining a virgin, than to conceive by concupiscence and to
bring forth in pain. On this side I behold a curse
indeed, yet no sin ; on that I see both sin † and torment.
Moreover, what is this curse but the reproach of men ?
For on no other account is she that is sterile declared
accursed than because she is held up to scorn and
contempt as being useless and unprofitable, and that
in Israel only. ' But for me it is a very small thing '
to incur the displeasure of men, provided I can present

* These exact words are not found in the Vulgate. In
Exodus xxiii. 26, we read, " There shall not be one fruitless
nor barren in thy land " ; and in Deuteronomy vii. 14, " No
one shall be barren among you of either sex "—(Translator).

† Sin is taken here in the same sense in which the Apostle
understands it where he says, " Now if I do that which I will
not, it is no more I that do it but sin that dwelleth in me "
(Rom. vii. 20), that is to say, for concupiscence —(Translator).

myself ' a chaste virgin to Christ.' "   O Virgin most
prudent, most devoted, who has told thee that virginity is pleasing to God ?   What law, what commandment, what page of the Old Testament either
enjoins, or counsels, or exhorts men to live in the flesh
without living according to the flesh, and to emulate
on earth the life of the angels ?   Where, O happy
Virgin, hast thou read that " the wisdom of the flesh
is death " ? or " Make not provision for the flesh in
its concupiscences " ?   Where hast thou read of
virgins that they shall sing a new canticle which none
but they can sing, and shall " follow the Lamb
whithersoever He goeth " ?   Where hast thou read
the eulogium pronounced on them " who have made
themselves eunuchs for the kingdom of heaven " ?
Where hast thou read that, " Though we walk in
the flesh, we do not war according to the flesh " ? or,
" Both he that giveth his virgin in marriage doth well,
and he that giveth her not doth better " ? Where
hast thou read, " I would that all men were even as
myself " ? or, " It is good for a man if he so continue (in virginity) according to my counsel " ? or,
" Concerning virgins I have no commandment of the
Lord, but I give counsel " ?   Thou hast had neither
counsel, nor command, nor example to guide thee, but
" His (Christ's) unction hath taught thee of all things,"
and the Word of God, " living and effectual," has been
thy Master before He became thy Son, and instructed
thy mind before assuming thy flesh.   Thou hast vowed,
therefore, to present thyself a chaste virgin to Christ,
not knowing that thou wert also destined to present
thyself to Him to be His Mother.   Thou hast chosen
to be contemptible in Israel, and, in order to please

Him to Whom thou hast devoted thyself, thou art content to incur the malediction pronounced against the sterile. But behold, the curse is changed into a blessing, and the purpose of barrenness is rewarded with motherhood.*

Prepare thyself now, O Virgin, expand thy breast and open thy bosom, "because He That is mighty" is going to do great things for thee, so that, instead of being accursed in Israel, "all generations shall call thee blessed." And fear not, O prudent Virgin, the fruitfulness offered thee, because it shall leave thy virginity inviolate. Thou shalt conceive, yet without concupiscence ; thou shall be pregnant, yet not burdened ; thou shalt bring forth, yet not with sadness ; thou shalt be a mother, yet know not man. But of whom shalt thou be mother ? Thou shalt be the Mother of Him Who has God for His Father. The Son of the Father's glory shall be the Crown of thy virginity. The Wisdom of the Father's Heart shall be the Fruit of thy virginal womb. In a word, thou shalt bring forth God and conceive by God. Be of good cheer, therefore, fruitful Virgin, chaste child-bearer (*puerpera*), Mother undefiled, because thou shalt

* "Though all Jewish women in each successive age had been hoping to be the Mother of the Christ, so that marriage was honourable among them, celibacy a reproach, she alone had put aside the desire and the thought of so great a dignity. She alone who was to bear the Christ refused to bear Him ; He stooped to her, she turned from Him ; and why ? because she had been inspired, the first of womankind, to dedicate her virginity to God, and she did not welcome a privilege which seemed to involve a forfeiture of her vow. How shall this be, she asked, seeing I am separate from man ? Nor, till the Angel told her that the conception would be miraculous and from the Holy Ghost, did she put aside her trouble of mind, recognise him securely as God's messenger, and bow her head in awe and thankfulness to God's condescension "—Newman, *Discourses to Mixed Congregations*, pp. 372-373.

no longer be accursed in Israel, or reputed with the
barren.   And if thou shalt continue to be cursed by
those who are Israelites according to the flesh, not
because they judge thee sterile, but from envy of thy
fruitfulness, remember that Christ also endured the
curse of the cross, and has blessed thee, His Mother,
in the glory of heaven.   Yea, even on earth thou art
declared blessed by the Angel, and all generations of
men shall justly call thee blessed.   Therefore, " Blessed
art thou among women, and blessed is the Fruit of
thy womb."

" Who, having heard, was troubled at his saying,
and thought with herself, what manner of salutation
this should be."   Virgins, who are truly such, are wont
to be always fearful, and can never feel secure.   And
in their anxiety to avoid all real danger, they tremble
at what is only an appearance.   For they know that
they carry their precious treasure " in earthen vessels,"
and that it is extremely difficult to live as angels
amongst men, to lead on earth the life proper to
heaven, and to live in the flesh without living according
to the flesh.   And consequently every strange event,
every unexpected occurrence, at once arouses their sus-
picions : they are afraid of a trap, they conclude it is
all an attempt against themselves.   Hence Mary was
troubled at the Angel's greeting.   She was troubled, I
say, but not confounded.   " I was troubled," sings the
Psalmist, " and I spoke not," but " I thought upon
the days of old, and I had in mind the eternal years."
In the same way, then, was Mary troubled and she
spoke not, but " thought with herself what manner of
salutation this should be."   That she was troubled
came from her virginal modesty ; that she was not

confounded was due to her fortitude, whilst it was under the influence of her prudence that she held her peace and reflected. " She was troubled and thought with herself what manner of salutation this should be." The prudent Virgin was well aware that the angel of darkness often transforms himself into an angel of light ; and as she was humble and simple, she could not believe that any holy angel would greet her thus. And therefore she " thought with herself what manner of salutation this should be."

Then the Angel, looking upon the Virgin, and easily perceiving that she is revolving anxious thoughts in her mind, consoles her timidity, dissipates her doubts, and familiarly addressing her by her name, tells her kindly not to be afraid. " Fear not, Mary," he says, " for thou hast found grace with God. There is here no guile and no deception. Do not suspect any artifice or treachery in me, because I am not a man but a spirit, and an angel not of Satan but of God. Fear not, Mary, for thou hast found grace with God. Oh, if thou knewest how pleasing thy humility is to the Most High and what a sublime throne of glory awaits thee in His kingdom ! Then thou wouldst no longer deem thyself unworthy to be saluted and served by angels. For how canst thou regard as undue to thee the love and devotion of the angels, seeing that thou hast found grace with God ? Thou hast found what thou hast been seeking, thou hast found what no one before thee has been able to find : ' thou hast found grace with God.' And what is this grace which thou hast found ? It is the reconciliation of men with God, the destruction of death, and the restoration of life. Yes, such is the grace thou hast found with God.

' And this shall be a sign to thee ' : ' behold thou shalt
conceive in thy womb, and shalt bring forth a Son,
and thou shalt call His name Jesus.'   From the very
name of the Son promised thee, thou mayest understand, O prudent Virgin, how precious and how extraordinary is the grace which thou hast found with God.
' And thou shalt call His name Jesus.' "   The same
Angel who spoke these words, gave also the meaning
of that name, as another Evangelist records, (Matth.
i. 21), interpreting it thus, " for He shall save His
people from their sins."

I have read of two others who, as types of Him
Whom the Angel here announces, bore the name of
Jesus and ruled in Israel.   One of them led the people
home from Babylon, whilst the other brought them into
the land of promise.   Both of these did indeed defend
those under them against the attacks of their enemies,
but did they save them from their sins ?   No, it is
only our Jesus Who can save His people from their
sins and bring them into the land of the living.   " For
He shall save His people from their sins."   " Who is
this that forgiveth sins also ? "   Oh, that the Lord
Jesus in spite of my unworthiness would vouchsafe to
count even me in the number of His people, that so I
might be saved from my sins !   Truly " happy is that
people whose God is the Lord " Jesus, because " He
shall save his people from their sins."   Yet there are
many, I fear, who proclaim themselves to belong to
His people, but whom He does not acknowledge.   I
fear there are many, even amongst those who seem
outwardly to be the most devoted of His people, of
whom nevertheless He is compelled to say, " This
people honoureth Me with their lips : but their heart is

far from Me." For "the Lord (Jesus) knoweth who are
His" in truth. He knows also whom He has chosen
from the beginning. "Why," He asks of some, "call
you Me Lord, Lord : and do not the things which I
say ? " Dost thou wish to know whether or not thou
belongest to His people ? Or rather dost thou desire
to belong to His people ? * If so, do the things which
Jesus says, and He will number thee with His people.
Do what the Lord Jesus commands in the Gospel,
what He commands in the law and the prophets, what
He commands by His ministers in the Church ; be
obedient to His representatives, thy superiors, " not
only to the good and gentle, but also to the froward,"
and learn from Jesus Himself to be meek and humble
of heart ; and then thou shalt be associated to that
blessed people, to " the people whom He hath chosen
for His inheritance " : thou shalt be of the noble people
" whom the Lord of Hosts hath blessed, saying, Thou
art the work of My hands, Israel is My inheritance." †
And concerning the same people (lest thou shouldst
grow envious of those who are Israelites according to the
flesh) He adds this other testimony, " A people whom
I knew not hath served Me : at the hearing of the
ear they have obeyed Me."

But let us hear now what the Angel thinks of Him
to Whom, before He is yet conceived, he has given a

* " Vis scire an pertineas ad populum Ejus ? Vel potius
vis esse de populo Ejus ? Fac quae dicit Jesus, et computabit
te in populo suo." These words recall the saying attributed
to St. Augustine, " Si non es praedestinatus, fac ut prae-
destineris," and prove beyond the possibility of a doubt that
St. Bernard subscribed to no theory of absolute and antecedent
predestination. See also the note at page 249, vol. i., of the
Sermons on the Canticle of Canticles —(Translator).

† This appears to be a reading of Isaias xix. 25, but differs
materially from both Septuagint and the Vulgate —(Translator).

name so noble. " He shall be great," he says, " and
shall be called the Son of the Most High." Great
indeed must be He Who shall deserve to be called
the Son of the Most High. Has He not a right to be
called great " of Whose greatness " according to the
Psalmist, " there is no end " ? And, as the same
Prophet elsewhere asks, " Who is the great God like
our God ? " Truly great is He Who is as great as
He is high, and Who is the Most High. For the Son
of the Most High " thinks it not robbery to be equal "
to the Most High. But *he* certainly must be judged to
have been guilty of robbery, who, having been elevated
from nothingness to the angelic dignity, compared
himself to his Maker, and attempted to usurp the prerogative of the Son of the Most High, the Son, not
made, but begotten by God the Father, as being
Himself in the form of God. For God the Father,
although Most High, although omnipotent, can nevertheless neither produce a creature equal to Himself,
nor generate a Son inferior to Himself. He made
Lucifer great indeed, yet not so great as He is Himself
and therefore not most high. The Only-Begotten Son
alone, Who has not been made, proceeds by generation
omnipotent from the Omnipotent, most high from the
Most High, eternal from the Eternal, Nor does the
Father think it robbery or injurious to His glory that
such a Son should be equal to Him in all things. Well,
therefore, is it said that He shall be great Who shall
be called the Son of the Most High.

But why does the Angel say that He shall be great,
and not rather that He is great ? For He is always
equally great and has no capacity for growth in
greatness : He shall not be anything greater after

conception than He is now, or than He has been in His
eternal past.   Perhaps the future tense is used to
indicate that He Who is already the great God is about
to become great also as man.   If this be so, Gabriel
speaks truly when he says, " He shall be great," that
is, a great Man, a great Doctor, a great Prophet ; for
such He is declared to be in the Gospel.   Thus we
read how the people said of Him, " A great Prophet
is risen up among us."   And a certain lesser prophet
promised that He would come as a great Prophet,
saying, " Behold a great Prophet shall come, and He
shall restore Jerusalem."   As for thee, O Virgin, thou
shalt bring Him forth as a Little One, thou shalt nurse
Him as a Little One, thou shalt suckle Him as a Little
One : but looking on His littleness, think of His greatness.   For He shall be great, because God will magnify
Him in the sight of princes so that " all the kings of
the earth shall adore Him, all nations shall serve Him."
Let thy soul, therefore, " magnify the Lord," because
" He shall be great and shall be called the Son of the
Most High."   He shall be great, and " He That is
mighty shall do great things to thee ; and holy is His
name."   For what name can be more holy than that
which He is to be called, the Son of the Most High ?
And let us also, who are little, magnify the great Lord,
Who in order that we might be made great, has made
Himself little.   " A Child is born to us," says the
Prophet, " and a Son is given to us."   He is born, I
say, for us, not for Himself : He Who is eternally and
far more nobly born of the Father had no need for
Himself of this temporal birth of a mother.   Neither is
it for the angels that He is born, because they possess
Him already as great, and hence do not need Him as

little. Therefore for us alone the Child is born and to us He is given, since to us alone is He necessary.

So let us now employ Him Who is born for us and given to us for the purpose for which He is born and given. Let us use Him Who is our own for our own advantage. Let us work out our salvation by means of the Saviour.* Behold a Little One is placed in our midst.† O Little One desirable to little ones! O Little One truly! but only little in malice, not in wisdom.‡ Let us endeavour to become like this Little One. Let us learn of Him because He is " meek and humble of heart." Otherwise the great God will have become a Little One in vain, in vain will have died, in vain will have endured the cross. Let us learn His humility, let us imitate His meekness, let us respond to His charity, let us share in His sufferings, let us cleanse ourselves in His Blood. Yea, let us offer Him as a " propitiation for our sins," because unto this is He born and given to us. Let us offer Him to the eyes of the Father : let us offer Him to His own eyes also : for the Father hath " spared not even His own Son, but delivered Him up for us all," and the Son hath " emptied Himself, taking the form of a servant " ; " He hath delivered His Soul unto death and was reputed with the wicked, and He hath borne the sins of many, and hath prayed for the transgressors," so that they might not perish. *They* cannot perish for

---

* " Utamur nostro in nostram utilitatem ; de Salvatore salutem operemur."

† " And Jesus, calling unto Him a little child, set him in the midst of them."—Matth. xviii. 2.

‡ Allusion to 1 Cor. xiv. 20 : " Brethren, do not become children in sense, but in malice be children, and in sense perfect."

whom the Son prays the Father that they may be saved, and for whom, that they may live, the Father delivered His Son to death. Pardon, therefore, is to be hoped for equally from Father and Son, Who are equal in mercy and loving-kindness, equal in omnipotence of will, identical in the Essence of their Divinity, in Which, with the Holy Spirit, They live and reign, one God, for ever and ever. Amen.

IV

FOURTH SERMON ON THE GLORIES OF THE VIRGIN MOTHER

" And the Lord God shall give unto Him the throne of David His father : and He shall reign in the house of Jacob for ever,
" And of His Kingdom there shall be no end.
" And Mary said to the Angel : How shall this be done, because I know not man ?
" And the Angel answering said to her : The Holy Ghost shall come upon thee, and the power of the Most High shall over-shadow thee. And therefore also the Holy which shall be born of thee shall be called the Son of God.
" And behold thy cousin Elizabeth, she also hath conceived a son in her old age ; and this is the sixth month with her that is called barren ;
" Because no word shall be impossible with God.
" And Mary said : Behold the handmaid of the Lord, be it done to me according to thy word "—Luke i. 32–38.

It is clear that the praise which we offer to the Mother redounds to the honour of the Son, and, conversely, when we glorify the Son we are at the same time honouring the Mother. For if, according to Solomon, " A wise son is the glory of his father," how much more glorious is it to be made the Mother of Him Who is Wisdom Itself ! But what shall I say in commendation of her whose glories have been foretold by the prophets, announced by the Angel, recorded by the Evangelist ? I shall not, therefore, because I dare not, attempt a eulogy of my own : I shall only repeat with devout affection that which the Evangelist has already proclaimed under the inspiration of the Holy Spirit. Continuing, then, we read, " And the Lord God shall give Him the throne of David His father." These also are the words of the Angel to the Virgin concerning the promised Son, assuring her that He is destined to obtain the kingdom of David. There is no doubt that the Lord Jesus truly belongs to the lineage of the Prophet King. But I ask, how did God give Him the throne of His father David, seeing that He never reigned in Jerusalem, aye, and even when the multitude on one occasion wished to make Him king, He would not consent ? Indeed, He distinctly affirmed before the face of Pilate that His kingdom was not of this world. Besides, it is surely nothing great to predict of Him Who " sitteth upon the Cherubims," Whom the Prophet Isaias saw " sitting upon a throne, high and elevated," that He should sit upon the throne of David, His father. But we know of another Jerusalem, typified by that earthly Jerusalem wherein David ruled, and far surpassing it in nobility and wealth. I think, therefore, that it is of this there is here question, according to the figure of speech so often met with in the Sacred Writings, by which the type is put for the thing typified. It was then, manifestly, that the Lord gave Him the throne of His father David, when, as the Psalmist tells us, He (Christ) was "appointed King by Him over Sion, His holy mountain." And this Prophet seems to explain clearly to what kingdom he is referring by the fact that he does not say " in Sion " but " over (*super*) Sion." For the reason why he uses the expression " over Sion " instead of " in Sion " seems to be this, that whereas David reigned *in* Sion, *over* Sion is the kingdom of Him of Whom God said to David, " Of the fruit of thy womb I will set over thy throne," and of Whom it was predicted by another prophet, " He shall sit over the throne of David, and over his kingdom." Do you not notice how the word " over " (*super*) is everywhere occurring ?

We have " over Sion," and " over thy throne," and
" over his kingdom."* Therefore, " the Lord God shall
give unto Him the throne of David His father," not
the typical throne but the true, not the temporal
but the eternal, not the earthly but the heavenly.
And this is said to be the throne of David, because,
as I have already remarked, it was prefigured by that
temporal throne on which David sat in Sion.

" And He shall reign in the house of Jacob for ever,
and of His Kingdom there shall be no end." Here
again, if the Angel be understood as referring to the
temporal house of Jacob, it may well be asked how
shall He reign for ever in a house which is not eternal?
We have consequently to seek for an eternal house
of Jacob, in which He shall reign for ever, of Whose
" kingdom there shall be no end." For was He not
impiously denied and foolishly rejected by that earthly
and provoking house, before the face of Pilate, to whose
question, " Shall I crucify your King ? " they all, with
one accord, cried out in answer, " We have no king
but Cæsar " ? Inquire, therefore, of the Apostle, and
he will distinguish for thee between the Jew " that
is so outwardly " and the Jew " that is one inwardly,"
between the circumcision " which is outward in the
flesh " and the circumcision which is " in the spirit,"
between the spiritual Israel and the carnal, between
the sons of Abraham's faith and the children of his
flesh. " For," he declares, " all are not Israelites that

* " Super Sion, super sedem, super solium, super regnum."
In order to preserve the Saint's meaning, I have uniformly
translated " super " by " over," even where the Douay Version,
renders it " upon." For to St. Bernard's mind the words
" De fructu ventris tui ponam super sedem tuam " are not
a promise that the Messias should occupy the throne of David,
but a throne above it in heaven —(Translator).

are of Israel ; neither are all they that are the seed of Abraham, children." Continue, then, according to this, and say, "similarly not all who are of Jacob are to be reputed of the house of Jacob." For Jacob and Israel are one and the same. Therefore consider none to belong to the house of Jacob except such as are found to be perfect in the faith of Jacob ; or rather recognise these as the spiritual and eternal house of Jacob, in which the Lord Jesus shall reign for ever. Where is the man amongst us who, according to the signification of the name Jacob, supplants the devil in his heart and struggles against his vices and concupiscences, so that sin may not reign in his mortal body, but that, instead, Jesus may reign in him, here by grace and hereafter by glory ? Oh, how blessed is he in whom Jesus shall reign for ever, because he also shall reign with Jesus, " and of his kingdom there shall be no end " ! Oh, how glorious is that kingdom in which " the kings of the earth shall assemble themselves and gather together " in order to praise and magnify Him Who is above all, " King of kings and Lord of lords," from the contemplation of Whose divine splendour " the just shall shine as the sun in the kingdom of their Father " ! Oh, if only the Lord Jesus would remember sinful me " in the favour of His people " when He comes into His kingdom ! Oh, if on that day when He is to " deliver up the kingdom to God and the Father," He would condescend to " visit (me) with His salvation, that (I) may see the good of His chosen, that (I) may rejoice in the joy of His nation, that He may be praised with His inheritance " even by me ! Meantime, " come, Lord Jesus," and remove all scandals from Thy kingdom, which is my poor soul, so that Thou Who art her rightful King, mayest reign in her. For avarice has entered and claims me for its own : vainglory desires to rule over me ; pride wishes to be my king ; sensuality says, " I will reign " ; ambition, envy, jealousy, and anger contend in me concerning myself, as to which of them shall have the greatest power over me. I resist them as well as I can : I struggle against them according as I am assisted by grace, I proclaim that the Lord Jesus is my only King. For Him I defend myself, because I acknowledge myself to be His subject. I adhere to Him as my Lord and my God, and I declare that I have no king but the Lord Jesus. Come, then, O Lord, and " scatter them by Thy power," that so Thou alone mayest reign in me, because " Thou art Thyself my King and my God, Who commandest the saving of Jacob."

"And Mary said to the Angel : How shall this be done, because I know not man ? " At first she prudently held her peace, whilst, still in doubt, she " thought with herself what manner of salutation this should be " ; for, being humble, she chose rather to answer nothing at all than rashly to say what she knew not. But now she has pondered the matter well and has been comforted, the Angel reassuring her exteriorly and God encouraging her interiorly—for He too is present to her, as the Angel has testified, saying, "The Lord is with thee." Therefore, being thus fortified, and having conquered fear by faith, and maidenly reserve by gladness, she asks the Angel, "How shall this be done, because I know not man ? " It is not that she doubts the fact : she only inquires concerning the means and the manner. For she does not ask " whether shall this be done ? " but, " How shall this

be done ? "   As if she should say, " Since my Lord,
Who is the witness of my conscience, knows that His
handmaid has vowed to preserve her virginity, by
what means and in what manner is He pleased that
this be done ?   Should it be necessary to set aside my
vow, in order to become the Mother of so great a Son,
I shall rejoice indeed because of the Son, but I shall
grieve at having to sacrifice my virginity : however,
may His will be done.   But if I am to conceive as a
virgin and to bring forth as a virgin,—which, if He so
please, is certainly within His power to accomplish—
then I shall know in truth that ' He hath regarded
the humility of His handmaid.' " *

" How shall this be done, because I know not man ?
And the Angel answering said to her : The Holy Ghost
shall come upon thee, and the power of the Most High
shall overshadow thee."   Already she has been declared full of grace ; and now it is said to her, " The
Holy Ghost shall come upon thee and the power of
the Most High shall overshadow thee."   But how can
she be full of grace without having the Holy Ghost,
since He is the Giver of all graces ?   And if the Holy
Ghost is already within her, what means this promise
of Him, as if He is to come upon heranew ?   Perhaps
we have the explanation of this difficulty in the fact
that the Angel does not simply say, " the Holy Ghost
shall *come* into thee " (*veniet in te*), but, " the Holy
Ghost shall ' *supervene* ' upon thee " (*superveniet in te*) ;
because He has come to her before with an abundance
of grace, and now it is announced that He shall
" supervene," on account of the fulness and super-

* Cf. A Lapide, *Comment. in Lucam*, c. i. 34 ; also St. Thomas,
Sum. Theol., III. q. xxx. a. 3.

abundance of grace which He is prepared to pour down upon her. But again, if she is already full of grace, how is she capable of receiving more? And if she has this capacity for further grace, how can she be said to be already full? Shall we suppose that the first fulness has filled her soul whilst the second is intended to fill her womb, so that the plenitude of the Divinity which even now dwells in her spiritually, as it has dwelt in many other holy persons, shall begin to dwell in her corporally also, a privilege accorded to no other saint?

The Angel therefore says, "The Holy Ghost shall come upon thee, and the power of the Most High shall overshadow thee." What does he mean by the words, "And the power of the Most High shall over-shadow thee"? Let him who can, comprehend them. But is there any creature—except perhaps her who alone merited to have in herself this most blessed experience—is there, I ask, any creature capable of comprehending with his intellect or of discerning by his reason how the inaccessible Splendour of the God-head poured Itself into the Virgin's womb, and how of that small portion of her body which It animated and united hypostatically to Itself, It made a shadow, as it were, for her whole being, in order that she might be able to endure the approach and the presence of such intolerable brightness? And possibly for this reason in particular it was said to her, "The power of the Most High shall overshadow thee," because, namely, the matter was thus shadowed in mystery, and because the knowledge of what the Blessed Trinity was pleased to accomplish, of Itself alone and directly, in and with the Virgin alone, was to be communicated to none except her to whom alone was to be granted the experience. In this sense, then, (as I suppose), the Angel said to her, " The Holy Ghost shall come upon thee "—in order by His presence to make thee fruitful, " and the power of the Most High shall overshadow thee," that is, " the manner in which thou shalt conceive by the Holy Ghost shall be so veiled and covered and overshadowed in His most secret counsel by Christ, the Wisdom and Power of God, that none shall have knowledge of it save Him and thee." It was as if Gabriel had answered the Virgin thus : " Wherefore askest thou me concerning that which thou art soon to experience in thyself ? Thou shalt know, thou shalt know, I say, and the knowledge shall fill thee with happiness : but none can instruct thee in this mystery except Him Who is its Author. My mission is not to effect but only to announce to thee thy virginal conception. And how this is to be accomplished, as it cannot be made known except by Him Who shall accomplish it, so neither can it be learned except by her in whom it shall be accomplished. And therefore also the Holy Which shall be born of thee shall be called the Son of God. That is to say, since it is not by man thou shalt conceive, but by the Holy Ghost, and since thou shalt conceive the Son of God, Who is the Power of the Most High, therefore also the Holy Which shall be born of thee shall be called the Son of God. I mean by this, that not only He Who (as being the Power of God) shall come from the Father's Bosom into thy womb and overshadow thee, but also whatever He shall unite to Himself of thy substance shall be called the Son of God : just as, on the other hand, He Who is born of the Father before all ages shall be reputed henceforth thy Son also. But in such a way shall the Son Who is born of the Father be thy Son, and the Son born of thee be the Son of the Father, that nevertheless there shall not be two Sons but one. And although there is an infinite difference between the Flesh Which this Son obtains from thee and the Divinity Which He derives from the Father, He shall not be only in part thy Son, and in part the Father's, but wholly and entirely the same Son of both thee and the Father." *

"And therefore also the Holy Which shall be born of thee shall be called the Son of God." Notice with what reverence the Angel said, " the Holy Which shall be born of thee." For wherefore did he speak of " the Holy " thus simply and without addition ? The reason is, as I believe, because he had no proper and suitable name for that most excellent, most magnificent, most venerable Something Which was to be taken from the Virgin's spotless flesh, and (with Its Soul) to be united to the Only-Begotten of the Father. Had he called It " the holy Flesh," or " the Sacred Humanity," or " the holy Infant," he would have seemed to himself

---

* That is to say, Christ is not merely the (natural) Son of God according to His Divinity and the Son of Mary according to His Humanity, but He is the Son of both His Father and His Mother according to His whole Self as the Word incarnate. " She (Mary) is not merely the Mother of Our Lord's manhood, or of Our Lord's Body, but she is also to be considered the Mother of the Word Himself, the Word incarnate. God in the Person of the Word, the Second Person of the All-glorious Trinity, humbled Himself to become her Son. ' Non horruisti Virginis uterum,' as the Church sings, ' Thou didst not shrink from the Virgin's womb.' He took the substance of His Human Flesh from her, and clothed in It lay within her, and He bore It about with Him after birth as a sort of badge and witness that He, though God, was hers."—Newman, *Discourses to Mixed Congregations*, p. 383.

Cf. St. Thomas, *Sum Theol.*, III. q. xxxv. a. 4-5 —(Translator).

to be speaking of It unworthily. He therefore referred to It indefinitely as " the Holy," because whatever That might be which was to be born of the Virgin, It was certainly Something holy and singularly holy, by the sanctification of the Spirit and by Its personal union with the Word.

"And behold thy cousin Elizabeth, she also hath conceived a son in her old age." Why was it necessary to announce to the Virgin that her hitherto sterile cousin had also conceived ? Is it that she was still perhaps doubtful, still hesitating to assent to the heavenly oracle, and therefore the Angel desired to convince her by the evidence of this other wonder ? God forbid ! We read of how Zachary's incredulity was punished by this same Angel, but nowhere do we find him reproving Mary for anything : rather we hear Elizabeth in the spirit of prophecy commending her faith and saying, " Blessed art thou that hast believed, because those things shall be accomplished that were spoken to thee by the Lord." No, the true reason why her cousin's pregnancy was announced to the Virgin was in order that her joy might be multiplied by hearing of such a succession of prodigies. For it was necessary that she, who was destined soon in the joy of the Holy Ghost to conceive the Son of the Father's charity, should be prevented and flooded with an unprecedented inundation of gladness and love ; because it was only the most loving and the most joyous of hearts that could contain Him Who is the infinite Treasure of divine love and sweetness. Or perhaps for this reason was Elizabeth's pregnancy made known to Mary, because it was manifestly fitting that the Virgin should hear from the Angel before learning from men a fact which was soon to be everywhere published. Otherwise it would have been thought that the Mother of God was excluded from the counsels of her Son, if she were kept in ignorance of what was taking place so near her on the earth. Or again, Mary may have been informed of her cousin's condition, to the end that, being notified now of the Saviour's, and now of the Precursor's coming, she might the better remember the time and order of the events, and so be better able to make known the truth afterwards to the apostles and evangelists, as one who had been fully and supernaturally enlightened concerning all these mysteries from the beginning. Or, finally, the purpose of telling the Virgin that Elizabeth had conceived may have been this : that the news of the elder cousin's condition might remind the younger of the claims of charity; so that the Virgin's hasty journey to the hill country to visit her kinswoman might afford the unborn Prophet an opportunity of rendering the first-fruits of his service to His still younger Lord ; and that, whilst the meeting of mothers and infants excited the joyous devotion of all, wonders should be followed by wonders more astonishing.

But, O Virgin, do not entertain the hope that these magnificent promises which thou hast heard from the Angel are to be fulfilled by him. And if thou wouldst know by whom, then, they shall be accomplished, attend to what the Angel adds, "Because no word shall be impossible with God." As if he should say, "For the fulfilment of the promises which I have faithfully made to thee, I presume not on my own strength, but on the power of Him Who has sent me ; because no word shall be impossible with God." For what word can be

impossible to Him Who has made all things by His Word?
Nevertheless I should like to know why the Angel did
not say, " because no *deed*" shall be impossible with
God, instead of, " because no word."   But perhaps he
preferred the latter expression, because as easily as
men can say what they will, even when they lack
the power of accomplishment, with the same ease, nay,
with incomparably greater ease, God is able to fulfil
in act whatever can be expressed in speech.   Let me
put it more plainly.   If it were as easy for men to
accomplish as to say what they will, then for us also
in the same way no deed would be impossible.   As
the case is, however, the familiar adage holds true,
namely, that there is a wide difference between doing
and saying, yet only for men, and not also for God.
For God alone it is the same thing to do as to say,
and the same thing to say as to will.   Consequently,
" no word shall be impossible with God."   To take an
example.   The prophets were able to foresee and to
foretell that the Virgin and her barren cousin would
conceive and bring forth : yet surely they had not
the power to bring to pass what they were capable of
announcing.   But God Who gave His prophets the
gift of foresight, with the same ease with which He
could predict what He pleased through them, could
afterwards, when He chose, accomplish by Himself
whatever He had promised.   For with God there can
be no discord between intention and promise, because
He is Truth ; nor between promise and accomplishment,
because He is Power ; nor between accomplishment and
mode, because He is Wisdom.   And consequently, " no
word shall be impossible with God."

O happy Virgin !   Thou hast heard what is to be

accomplished in thee, and what is to be the mode of accomplishment. Each is a matter for wonder, yet also and equally an occasion of joy. Therefore, "rejoice greatly, shout for joy, O Daughter of Jerusalem." And since "to thy hearing has been given joy and gladness," let us also hear from thee the reply of gladness which we so eagerly long for; and then "the bones that have been humbled shall rejoice." Thou hast heard, I say, what is to be accomplished in thee, and thou hast believed; believe also what has been explained to thee concerning the mode of accomplishment. Thou hast been told that thou shalt conceive and bear a Son: thou hast heard that this shall be not by man but by the operation of the Holy Spirit. Behold the Angel now awaits thy answer: "it is time that he should return to the Lord Who sent him." We also, O Lady, await from thy lips the sentence of mercy and compassion, we who are so miserably groaning under the sentence of condemnation. For lo! the price of our salvation is now offered to thee: if thou wilt only consent, we shall at once be set at liberty. We have been created by the eternal Word of God, and behold we die: by thy momentary word we must be renewed and restored to life. O Virgin most loving, Adam, now exiled from Paradise with all his miserable offspring, implores this favour of thee. For this does Abraham entreat thee, for this David, for this all the other holy fathers, thine own ancestors, who are now dwelling in the region of the shadow of death. See, the whole world, prostrate at thy feet, awaits thy answer. And not without cause. For on thy word depend the consolation of the miserable, the redemption of the captives, the pardon of the condemned, the

salvation of all the children of Adam, of the entire
human race. O Virgin, delay not to answer. Speak
the word, O Lady, speak the word which all on earth,
and all in limbo, yea, and even all in Paradise are
waiting to hear. Christ Himself, the King and Lord
of all, longs for thy answer with a longing equal to
the ardour wherewith He "hath desired thy beauty,"
because it is by means of thy consent that He has
decreed to save the world. Hitherto thou hast pleased
Him by thy silence, but now thy speech shall give
Him more pleasure. For behold He calls to thee from
heaven, saying, " O fairest among women, let thy
voice sound in My ears." Therefore if thou wilt give
Him to hear thy voice, He will give thee to see our
salvation. And is it not for this thou hast been sup-
plicating, and sighing, and pouring out prayers with
tears by day and by night ? What then ? Art thou she
to whom this hath been promised " or look we for
another ? " Nay, thou thyself art she, and there is
none other. Thou, I say, art she who has been promised, who has been expected, who has been yearned
for, through whom the holy Patriarch Jacob hoped to
receive eternal life, when, being now about to die, he
exclaimed, " I will look for Thy salvation, O Lord."
Thou art she in whom and by whom " God our King
before the ages hath decreed to work salvation in the
midst of the earth." Wherefore dost thou expect
from another what is now offered to thyself ? Why
hopest thou to receive through another that which
through thee shall be soon given to the world, provided only thou wilt consent and say the word ?
Make haste, therefore, to answer the Angel, or rather
to answer the Lord through the Angel. Say the word

and receive the Word. Utter thy human word and conceive the Divine Word. Pronounce the transitory word and embrace the Word everlasting. Why dost thou hesitate ? Wherefore dost thou fear ? Believe, consent, and receive into thy womb the Word of the Father. Let thy humility take courage, let thy modesty be confident. It is in nowise expedient now that thy virginal simplicity should be forgetful of prudence. O Virgin most prudent, in this matter alone thou mayest put aside all fear of presumption, because although modesty pleases by its silence, yet more necessary for us now is the charity of speech. O happy Virgin, open thy heart to faith, open thy lips to consent, open thy bosom to thy Creator. Behold the Desired of all nations is standing outside and knocking at thy door. Oh, if He should pass on whilst thou delayest to open, and thou shouldst have to begin once more to seek with sorrow " Him Whom thy soul loveth " ! Arise, therefore, and make haste to open to Him. Arise by faith, make haste by devotion, open by consent.

" And Mary said : Behold the handmaid of the Lord, be it done to me according to thy word." Divine grace is always found in intimate union with the virtue of humility, because " God resisteth the proud and giveth grace to the humble." The Virgin therefore replies with humility, in order that the seat of grace may be prepared in her. " Behold," she says, " the handmaid of the Lord." Oh, how sublime is the humility here manifested, which knows not how to yield to honour or to be elated with glory ! She is chosen to be the Mother of God, and she calls herself His handmaid ! Assuredly it is a sign of a more than common humility not to forget humility in the presence of such glory. To be humble in abjection is nothing very great ; but it is great virtue indeed, and as rare as great, to be humble in the midst of honours. For instance, were the Church, deceived by my hypocrisy, to advance such a miserable wretch as I to some post of honour, even though not very exalted, God permitting this either on account of my own sins or because of the sins of those under me : should I not immediately forget what I really am and begin to suppose myself such as I am reputed by men, who cannot see the heart ? Undoubtedly : I should give credit to public opinion, and turn a deaf ear to the voice of conscience. And estimating virtue by honour, not honour by virtue, I should account myself the more holy in proportion as I should find myself elevated above others. You may see very many now in the Church, who, after being raised from a mean condition to honourable rank, and from penury to affluence, have become suddenly inflated with pride and forgetful of their former abjection, so much so indeed that they are ashamed of their kindred, yea, even disdain to acknowledge their humble parents. You may also see some wealthy persons aspiring to all kinds of ecclesiastical honours ; and then, having changed their dress without changing their morals, they congratulate themselves on their sanctity. They deem themselves worthy of the positions which they have obtained by intrigue, and attribute to merit the honours which (if I may venture to affirm it) they have purchased for money. However, I will say nothing more about such as these, who are blinded by ambition, and to whom honourable positions furnish occasions for pride.

But there are others to be seen, who (I grieve to say it), after despising the glory of earthly pomp, appear to have learned pride in the very school of humility, and in the cloister itself, under the wings of the meekest and humblest of masters, to have become more arrogant and impatient than ever they were in the world. And what carries perversity further still, many are unable to put up with the least contempt in religion, who, whilst living in the world, could make themselves appear nothing better than contemptible. Their motive for entering the cloister would seem to be this, that since there was no chance of honours for them where honours were sought for by others, *there* at least they might hope for some honours where such things were avoided by all but themselves. Yet others I see—and the sight is an afflicting one—who, after entering the army of Christ, entangle themselves again in worldly affairs, again give themselves up to earthly solicitudes. You may behold them displaying much zeal in the building of houses, whilst they neglect the care of their conscience. Under the pretext of the common good, they sell their words to the wealthy and their greetings to matrons ; aye, and contrary to the edict of their Divine Emperor, they covet the goods of others, and contentiously strive to recover their own, not attending to the Apostle, who announces in the name of his Sovereign ; " Already indeed there is plainly a fault among you, that you have lawsuits one with another. Why do you not rather suffer yourselves to be defrauded ? " Is it thus *they* have crucified the world to themselves and themselves to the world, who, whereas they were once scarcely known in their own hamlet or village, now passing from province to

province and from court to court, are reckoned amongst
the acquaintance of kings and the familiars of princes?
What shall I say of the religious habit itself, which
they no longer esteem for its worth even as a com-
fortable covering, but only for its value as a graceful
ornament? And they pay more attention to the
material habit which clothes their bodies than to the
moral habits of their minds. It is a shocking thing to
say : the vain woman is now outdone in her own
special art by the religious who looks more to costliness
in matters of dress than to use or necessity. Even
the outward form of religion is discarded by these
soldiers of Christ, who value its livery not as a protection for their souls but as a becoming decoration
for their bodies,—who, when they ought to prepare
themselves for battle and to advance against the
" powers of the air " beneath the banner of poverty
(which the adversary so greatly fears) prefer in their
soft garments to exhibit the sign of peace, and thus
voluntarily, and without striking a blow, place themselves helpless in the hands of their enemies. The
cause of such dreadful evils is to be found in the fact
that the humility through which we abandoned the
world has itself been abandoned by us, with the
consequence that we are compelled once more to
pursue the vain objects of worldly ambition, becoming
as dogs that go back to the vomit.

Let us, therefore —I mean all who recognise themselves as belonging to this class—let us listen, I say,
to the answer of her who, even when she was chosen to
be the Mother of God, did not lose sight of humility. " Behold the handmaid of the Lord," she replied,
" be it done to me according to thy word." The words

" be it done to me " are an expression not of doubt but of desire. Hence, when she says, " be it done to me according to thy word," we must understand her as giving utterance to an ardent wish, and not as requiring proof after the manner of the incredulous. Nevertheless, it is also possible to regard these words as a prayer, since no one ever prays for anything unless because he has faith and hopes to receive it. And God wills that we should pray to Him even for what He has promised. Perhaps the reason why He first promises what He designs to bestow is in order that the promise may excite our devotion, and that thus what should otherwise be given gratuitously, may now be rendered as the reward of devout supplication. So does our loving Lord, Who desires that all men should be saved, endeavour to extort merits for us from ourselves ; and He prevents us by bestowing upon us gratuitously what He may reward, because otherwise the reward itself should be given gratuitously. The prudent Virgin was not ignorant of this when to the prevenient grace of gratuitous promise she joined the merit of fervent petition, praying, " Be it done to me according to thy word." As if she should say, " Concerning the Word of the Father be it done to me according to thy word. According to thy word, let the Word Who was in the beginning with God be made flesh of my flesh. Let the Word, I pray, become to me not as a spoken word which passes away, but a Word conceived and abiding; a Word enclosed in a body of flesh, not a word expressed by the sound of the voice. Let Him become to me not an audible word which sounds in the ear, but a visible Word that my eyes may see Him, a tangible Word that my hands may hold Him, a portable Word that I may carry Him in my arms. And let Him not become for me a written and silent word, but a Word incarnate and living : that is to say, not a word inscribed in dumb characters upon dead parchment, but the Word of God in human form impressed upon the living page of my chaste bosom, impressed, I say, not by the agency of mortal hand, but by the operation of the Holy Spirit. Let Him become to me what He has become to none before and shall become to none after me. God ' at sundry times and in divers manners spoke in times past to the fathers by the prophets,' and the Word of the Lord is said to have come to the mouth of some, to the ear of some others, and even to the hand of other some : but my prayer is that, according to thy word, He would vouchsafe to come into my womb. I do not ask that He should be orally proclaimed to me, or that He should be symbolically represented, but that He be silently infused, personally incarnated, corporally enclosed. Therefore let the Word of God, Who in Himself has neither the need nor the power to be made, let Him, I pray, condescend to be made flesh in me and for me, according to thy word. According to thy word, let Him be made flesh for the whole world, but in a more particular manner for me." *

* The Saint is here taking the words " fiat mihi secundum verbum tuum " to mean ; Let him (the Word) be made (flesh) for me according to thy word. It is the teaching of holy and enlightened men that the Incarnation was more for Mary's sake than for all the world beside —(Translator).

V

SERMON FOR THE FEAST OF THE NATIVITY OF THE BLESSED VIRGIN MARY

(SEPTEMBER 8)

" My Beloved to me and I to Him Who feedeth among the lilies till the day break and the shadows retire "—Cant. ii. 16, 17.

Heaven rejoices to-day in the presence of the Virgin Mother and her memory is revered upon earth. So it is, my brethren, because to the blessed above belongs the actual possession of all good, whilst we have to be content with the memorials thereof ; their portion is the fulness of bliss, ours but a taste of the first-fruits ; they exult in the vision of the glory of God, we in His name. " Thy name, O Lord, is for ever," sings the Psalmist, " Thy memorial, O Lord, from generation to generation" (Ps. cxxxiv. 13). Mark the expression, " from generation to generation." This evidently applies not to the holy angels but to men. Do you wish to know for certain that we have here on earth only the name and the memorial of God and that His presence is exhibited above ? "Thus, therefore, shall you pray," said Christ, " Our Father Who art in heaven, hallowed be Thy name " (Matt. vi. 9). This is in truth the " prayer of faith," (James. v. 15), the opening words of which remind us of our adoption as the children of God and admonish us that the earth is but the place of our pilgrimage ; so that " knowing that while we are in the body we are absent from the Lord " (2 Cor. v. 6), we may begin to " groan within

79

ourselves, waiting for the adoption of the sons of God "
(Rom. viii. 23), waiting for the presence of the Father.
It is with the same significance, therefore, the Psalmist
says, speaking even of Christ, " A spirit before our
face is Christ the Lord ; under His shadow we shall
live among the Gentiles" (Jer. Lam. iv. 20, juxta LXX).
" Among the gentiles," yes, but not among the blessed
angels : for there we shall live no longer under His
shadow, but in the full splendour of His divine glory.
" In the splendours of the saints, from the womb before
the day-star I begot Thee " (Ps. cix. 3) : but these,
as you know, are the words of the Heavenly Father
addressed to His only begotten Son.

It was under the shadow, not in the splendour,
that the same Son was brought forth by His Mother,
yet under no other shadow than that wherewith the
Most High Himself overshadowed her (Luke i. 35).
Rightly, therefore, does the Church sing—not the
Church of the saints triumphant, which is above,
amid the splendours of the saints, but that which
is as yet in banishment here below—" I sat down
under His shadow Whom I desired, and His fruit
was sweet to my palate " (Cant. ii. 3). She had
requested of the Bridegroom that He would show
her the meridian brightness wherein He feedeth (Cant.
i. 6), but her petition was refused, and instead of
the fulness of light she obtained only the shadow :
instead of the satiety she longed for she was given
a foretaste. Notice how she does not say, " I sat
down under His shadow *which* I desired," but, " under
His shadow *Whom* I desired." For it was not the
shadow she had so eagerly asked for, but the
meridian splendour, the perfect light of the Perfect

Light. " And His fruit," she adds, " was sweet to
my palate," that is, " to my taste." " How long wilt
Thou not spare me, nor suffer me to swallow down
my spittle ? " (Job vii. 19). How long must I be
satisfied with what Thou offerest in the words, " Taste
and see that the Lord is sweet " (Ps. xxxiii. 9) ? Thy
fruit, nevertheless, is sweet to the palate and delightful
to the taste, so that even for this much the Spouse
had good reason to break forth into the voice of
thanksgiving and praise (Is. li. 3).

But when shall it be said to us, " Eat, O friends,
and drink, and be inebriated, my dearly beloved "
(Cant. v. 1) ? " Let the just feast," sings the Psalmist,
but above " in the sight of God " (Ps. lxvii. 4), and
not here below under the shadow. And the same
Prophet says of himself, " I shall be satisfied when
Thy glory shall appear " (Ps. xvi. 15). The Lord
Jesus also thus addressed His apostles : " You are
they who have continued with Me in My temptations ;
and I dispose to you, as My Father hath disposed to
Me, a kingdom, that you may eat and drink at My
table." But where, O Lord ? " In My kingdom "
(Luke xxii. 28-30). Truly " blessed is he that shall
eat bread in the kingdom of God " (Luke xiv. 15).
" Hallowed," therefore, " be Thy name " by which
" Thou, O Lord, art among us " even now whilst we
abide upon earth, " dwelling by faith in our hearts "
(Ephes. iii. 17), for even now " Thy name is called
upon by us " (Jer. xiv. 9). And may " Thy kingdom
come " (Matt. vi. 10). Yea, let that kingdom " which
is perfect " come, and let " that which is in part be
done away " (1 Cor. xiii. 10). " Now," says the
Apostle, " you have your fruit unto sanctification,

and the end life everlasting " (Rom. vi. 22). Life
everlasting ! A never-failing fountain which irrigates
the whole extent of the paradise of God ! And not
merely does it irrigate : it floods, that " fountain of
gardens, the well of living waters which run with a
strong stream from Libanus " (Cant. iv. 15) ; it is the
river the stream whereof " maketh the city of God
joyful " (Ps. xlv. 5).

Now what is this fountain of life if it be not Christ the
Lord ? " When Christ shall appear Who is your life,"
says the Apostle, " then you also shall appear with
Him in glory " (Col. iii. 4). Truly He Who is the
fulness of all good emptied Himself (Phil. ii. 7) in order
to be " made unto us justice and sanctification and redemption " (1 Cor. i. 30), although not yet appearing as
our life, our glory, or our beatitude. For the " Fountain
is conveyed abroad " in a stream even to us ; Its
waters flow " in the streets," although " the stranger
partake not of them " (Prov. v. 16, 17). This stream
from the heavenly source descends to us through an
Aqueduct ; it does not indeed exhibit all the fulness
of the Fountain, but it serves to moisten our dry and
withered hearts with some few drops of the waters
of grace, giving more to one, less to another. The
Aqueduct itself is always full, so that all may receive
of its fulness (John i. 16), yet not the fulness itself.

You have already divined, dearest brethren, unless
I mistake, to whom I allude under the image of an
Aqueduct which, receiving the fulness of the Fountain
from the Father's heart, has transmitted the same
to us, if not as it is in itself, at least in so far as we
could contain it. Yea, for you know to whom it was
said, " Hail, full of grace " (Luke ii. 28). But shall

we not wonder how such and so great a Conduit could
have been formed, the top of which—like the ladder
which Jacob saw in vision (Gen. xxviii. 12)—was to
reach to heaven, nay, to be lifted higher than the
heavens, and to touch that Living Fountain of " the
waters that are above the heavens " (Ps. cxlviii. 4) ?
Even Solomon wondered at this, and, as if despairing
of the possibility, cried out, " who shall find a valiant
woman " (Prov. xxxi. 10) ?   In fact the reason why
the streams of heavenly grace did not begin to flow
down upon the human race for so long a time was
this : that the precious Conduit whereof I speak did
not as yet mediate between God and man.   Nor shall
we be surprised that it was awaited for so many ages
if we but remember how many years the just man
was employed in building an ark " wherein a few,
that is eight souls, were saved by water " (1 Peter
iii. 20), and that only for a very short time.

But how did this Conduit of ours, this " valiant
Woman," attain to the loftiness of the Fountain ?
How indeed, save by the ardour of her desires, by the
fervour of her devotion, by the purity of her prayer ?
For it is written, " The prayer of a just man pierceth
the clouds " (Ecclus. xxxv. 21).   And who is just if
not Mary, from whom the very Sun of justice has arisen
upon us ?   How, then, did she reach up even to the
inaccessible Majesty but by knocking, by asking, by
seeking ? (Matt. vii. 7).   Yea, and she found what
she was seeking, since to her it was said, " Thou hast
found grace with God " (Luke i. 30). What ?   She was
already " full of grace " and has she found yet more
grace ?   Oh, she indeed deserved to find what she
sought who was not satisfied with her own plenitude

nor content with her own abundance, but, according to that which is written, " They that drink Me shall yet thirst " (Ecclus. xxiv. 29)—solicited a super-abundance that might suffice for the salvation of all. Hence the Archangel reassured her, saying, " The Holy Ghost shall come upon thee " (ibid. 35) and shall infuse into thy heart the precious balsam of His grace with such overflowing prodigality that it shall stream out on every side. So in truth it is, my brethren, such has been our own experience. For now at last are our " faces made cheerful with oil " (Ps. ciii. 15). Now we have begun to exclaim, " Thy name is as oil poured out " (Cant. i. 2) and " Thy memorial, O Lord, from generation to generation." Neither has this overflow been in vain : the oil poured out has not been wasted, since therefore even " young maidens," that is, souls young in virtue, have learned to love the Bridegroom " exceedingly" (Cant. i. 2), and the precious ointment, running down from the Head, has been communicated not alone to the beard, but even to the skirts of the garment (Ps. cxxxii. 2).

Behold, O man, the counsel of God ; acknowledge the counsel of His wisdom, the counsel of His love. Designing to irrigate the floor with the dew of heaven, the Lord first poured down upon the fleece all the precious liquid (Judges vi. 37) : designing to redeem the human race He placed the whole ransom in the hands of Mary. Wherefore this ? Possibly in order that Mother Eve might be excused by her Daughter, and that the complaint of the man against the woman might be hushed for evermore. Never again, O Adam, never again shalt thou say to God, " The woman whom Thou gavest me to be my companion gave me of the forbidden fruit " (Gen. iii. 12) ; but rather let thy words be henceforth : " The woman whom Thou gavest me fed me with the fruit of benediction." Here indeed we have a counsel full of love. But perchance we have not yet seen it all, perchance something remains still to be discovered. That which I have told you is true undoubtedly, yet—unless I am deceived—it is not enough to satisfy your desires. You have enjoyed the sweetness of the milk : perhaps if we labour the subject a little more we shall succeed in extracting therefrom the fatness of the butter.

Let us, therefore, look more deeply into this matter, and let us see with what sentiments of tender devotion the Lord would have us honour Mary, in whom He has placed the plenitude of all good ; so that if there is anything of hope in us, if anything of grace, if anything of salvation, we may feel assured it has overflowed unto us from her who " went up from the desert flowing with delights " (Cant. viii. 5). Oh, truly may we call her a garden of delights, which the Divine " South Wind " not merely " comes and blows upon " (Cant. iv. 16), but comes down into and blows through, causing its aromatical spices, that is, the precious gifts of heavenly grace, to flow out and to be diffused abroad on every side. Remove from the heavens the material sun which enlightens the world, and what becomes of the day ? Remove Mary, remove this Star of the sea, of life's " great and spacious sea " (Ps. ciii. 25), and what is left us but a cloud of involving gloom, and " the shadow of death " (Job x. 22), and a darkness exceeding dense ?*

* This paragraph with a portion of the following is used for the lessons of the Votive Office of the Blessed Virgin in the Cistercian Breviary —(Translator).

Therefore, my dearest brethren, with every fibre, every feeling of our hearts, with all the affections of our minds, and with all the ardour of our souls, let us honour Mary, because such is the will of God, Who would have us to obtain everything through the hands of Mary. Such, I say, is the will of God, but intending our advantage. For exercising a provident care for us, her poor children, in all things and through all things, the Virgin Mother calms our trembling fear, enlivens our faith, strengthens our hope, drives away our distrust, raises up our pusillanimity. Thou wast afraid, O man, to approach the Father; thou wast terrified at the mere sound of His voice, and soughtest to conceal thyself amongst the foliage (Gen. iii. 8). Therefore He gave thee Jesus as thy Mediator. What shall not such a Son be able to obtain for thee from such a Father? Doubtless He shall be " heard for His reverence " (Heb. v. 7) : for " the Father loveth the Son " (John iii. 35). Surely thou art not afraid of approaching Him also? " He is thy Brother and thy flesh " (Gen. xxxvii. 27), " tempted in all things like as thou art, but without sin " (Heb. iv. 15), " that He might become merciful " (Heb. ii. 17). Him Mary has given thee for thy Brother. But perhaps thou standest in awe of the Divine Majesty of Jesus? For although He has become man He has not ceased to be God. Perhaps thou desirest to have an advocate even with Him? If so, have recourse to Mary. In Mary human nature is found entirely pure, not alone pure from all defilement, but pure also from composition with another nature. Nor do I deem it doubtful that she likewise shall be heard for her reverence. Assuredly the Son will listen to the Mother and the

Father will listen to the Son. My little children, behold the sinner's ladder, behold the main source of my confidence, the principal ground of my hope. What? Can the Son refuse aught to His own Mother or be refused aught by His Father? Can the Son deny a hearing to her or be denied a hearing by Him? Both suppositions are plainly impossible. "Thou hast found grace with God," said the Archangel to Mary. Happy Virgin! Yes, dearest brethren, Mary shall always find grace with God, and grace alone is what we have need of. Prudent Virgin! she does not ask either wisdom, as did Solomon (3 Kings iii. 9), or riches, or honours, or power, but only grace. For it is by grace alone we shall be saved.

Wherefore then should we desire anything else? My brethren, let us seek grace and let us seek it through Mary. Through Mary, I say, because she always finds what she seeks and can never suffer a disappointment. Yes, let us seek grace, but " grace with God," for with men " grace is deceitful " (Prov. xxx. 31). Others may seek after merit, but let it be our endeavour to find grace. Why should it not be so? Is it not grace that has brought us hither? Undoubtedly, it is " the mercy of the Lord that we are not consumed " (Jer. Lam. iii. 22). For what are we? What but so many sinners, so many perjurers, murderers, robbers : what but " the refuse of this world and the offscouring of all? " (1 Cor. iv. 13).*

---

* This, of course, must not be taken literally, but in a spiritual sense : as in Sermon III. for the Epiphany we are told that to resist the inspirations of grace is to join with Herod and Pharao in slaughtering the Hebrew innocents. In the same way, any slight infidelity or feeling of vanity may be viewed as participating in the malice of perjury or theft. Or perhaps the holy Preacher had in mind the words of St.

Look into your own consciences, my brethren, and
see that "where sin abounded grace hath abounded
more" (Rom. v. 20). Mary did not presume on her
merit but solicited grace. Indeed she depended so
much upon grace and was so far from being "high-
minded" (Rom. xi. 20) that the Angel's salutation
alarmed her. "She was troubled at his saying and
thought with herself what manner of salutation this
should be" (Luke i. 29). For she considered herself
unworthy of this angelic greeting, and we may fancy
her asking herself in the words of Elizabeth, "Whence
is this to me that the Angel of my Lord should
come to me?" (ibid. 43). But "fear not, Mary"
(ibid. 30), and be not surprised at the coming of the
Angel, for One greater than even Gabriel has come
to thee. Wonder not at the presence of the Angel
of the Lord, for the Lord of the Angel is also with
thee. And, after all, what wonder is it that the Angel
should show himself to thee who art already living an
angelic life? What wonder is it that the Angel should
visit one whose life is as heavenly as his own? What
wonder, I say, that the Angel should salute "the
fellow-citizens with the saints and the domestics of
God" (Ephes. ii. 19)? For undoubtedly to live as
a virgin is to lead an angelic life; and they who neither
marry nor are given in marriage "shall be as the
angels of God" (Matt. xxii. 30).

You perceive now, my brethren, that in this manner
likewise our Aqueduct reached up to the Fountain of
grace; that it was not by her prayer alone that Mary

Augustine : "There is no sin committed by any man which
another would not also commit unless restrained by the grace
of God" (Hom. 23) —(Translator).

penetrated the heavens, but also by her incorruption, which, according to the Wise Man, " bringeth near to God " (Wisdom vi. 20). For she certainly was a " virgin holy in body and in spirit " (1 Cor. vii. 34), who had a better right than any other mere mortal to say, " Our conversation is in heaven " (Phil. iii. 20). Yes, " holy in body and in spirit," so that there might be no room for suspicion with regard to our Aqueduct. Exceedingly high though it is, it has preserved its integrity inviolate. This Virgin is in truth " a garden enclosed, a fountain sealed up " (Cant. iv. 12), the living temple of the Lord, the sanctuary of the Holy Spirit. No foolish virgin is Mary, for not alone is she possessed of oil, but she has all the fulness of the oil stored up in her vessel (Matt. xxv. 3). " In her heart she hath disposed to ascend by steps " (Ps. lxxxiii. 6), mounting up not merely by her prayer, but also, as I have said, by the holiness of her conversation. Moreover, she " went into the hill country with haste and saluted Elizabeth " and remained ministering to her " about three months " (Luke i. 39, 40, 56) ; so that the Mother could have said then what the Son shall say long after : " Suffer it to be so now, for so it becometh us to fulfil all justice " (Matt. iii. 15). Here indeed we behold her ascending the hill country, ascending the mystical mountains, for her " justice is as the mountains of God " (Ps. xxxv. 7). And so we have here the Virgin's third mode of ascent, the third strand of the " threefold cord " which " is not easily broken " (Eccles. iv. 12). Charity burned brightly in her seeking after grace, virginity shone resplendent in the immaculate purity of her flesh, whilst humility appeared sublime in her ministrations

to her cousin. I say, her humility appeared sublime :
because if " he that humbleth himself shall be exalted " (Matt. xxiii. 12), what can there be more
sublime than the humility of Mary ? Elizabeth was
surprised to see her coming and exclaimed, " Whence
is this to me that the Mother of my Lord should come
to me ? " But let her be more surprised now when
she learns that the Mother, like her Son, " has come
not to be ministered unto but to minister " (Matt. xx.
28). Good reason therefore had the inspired singer,
prophesying of Mary, to cry out in admiration, " who
is she that ascendeth * as the morning rising, fair as
the moon, bright as the sun, terrible as an army set
in array ? " (Cant. vi. 9). She ascended indeed above
the whole human race, she ascended even to the angelic
choirs, yea, even these she left beneath her and soared
high aloft above the whole celestial creation. For
she must needs mount beyond the heavenly host in
order to draw that living water which it is her destined
office to pour down upon men.

" How shall this be done," she inquired of the Angel,
" because I know not man ? " (Luke i. 34). Oh, in
truth she was " holy in body and in spirit," since, as
her words imply, she was then a virgin inviolate with
the purpose of always preserving her virginity intact.
But the Angel in answer said to her, " The Holy
Ghost shall come upon thee and the power of the Most
High shall overshadow thee " (ibid. 35). Which may
be paraphrased thus : " Do not ask me, O Virgin, how

* " Ascendit "—a reading I have been able to find nowhere
else. The Vulgate has " progreditur," whilst in the Greek we
find " ἐκκύπτουσα," " peeping forth," more appropriate to the
dawn—(Translator).

the divine purpose shall be accomplished ; ' It is high
and I cannot reach it ' (Ps. cxxxviii. 6). ' the Holy
Ghost, not any created spirit, ' shall come upon thee,
and,' not I, but ' the power of the Most High shall
overshadow thee.' " Be not content, O holy Virgin,
to take thy stand even amongst the blessed angels ;
for the thirsting earth hopes to receive through thy
hands a more excellent draught than it could ever
expect from angelic ministrations. When thou hast
passed a little beyond them, thou shalt find Him Whom
thy soul loveth (Cant. iii. 4). I say "a *little* beyond
them," not as forgetting that the Lord is exalted
infinitely above His angelic creatures, but to signify
the fact that between Him and them is found no intermediary. Ascend, therefore, O Virgin, above the
Virtues and the Dominations, above the Cherubim also
and the Seraphim ; ascend to the very presence of
Him of Whom they sing with mighty voice from choir
to choir, " Holy, holy, holy is the Lord God of hosts "
(Is. vi. 3). " And therefore also the Holy Which shall
be born of thee shall be called the Son of God " (Luke
i. 35). The Fountain of wisdom is the Word of the
Father Who dwelleth on high. This Divine Word
will become man, O Virgin, through thy co-operation,
so that He Who can say, " I am in the Father and
the Father is in Me " (John xiv. 10) may be able to
say also, " From God I have proceeded and come "
(John viii. 42). " In the beginning was the Word "
(John i. 1). Even then Wisdom's Well was full, but
as yet only unto Itself. Hence the Evangelist immediately adds, " and the Word was with God "
(ibid.), dwelling doubtless in " light inaccessible "
(1 Tim. vi. 16). The Lord, too, even in the beginning,

was " thinking towards us thoughts of peace and not of affliction " (Jer xxix. 11).   But, O Lord, these thoughts of Thine are hidden in Thy mind and we know not what sentiments Thou entertainest towards us. " For who hath known the mind of the Lord ? Or who hath been His counsellor ? " (Rom. xi. 34).   Therefore did Thy thoughts of peace materialise at last in works of peace : therefore was the Word made flesh and dwelleth among us (John i. 14) even now. Yes, He dwelleth "even now by faith in our hearts." (Ephes. iii. 17), He dwelleth in our memory, He dwelleth in our thought ; He even descends so far as to dwell in our imagination.

Before the incarnation, how could man conceive any image at all of his Maker, unless perchance he represented Him in his heart under the image of an idol ? For God was then unimaginable and inaccessible. He was altogether beyond the reach of sight and sensible conception.   But now He would be better known, He would make Himself an object as well to our eyes as to our intellects. How so, do you ask ? By showing Himself to us lying in the manger, reposing on His Virgin Mother's lap, preaching on the mountain, passing the night in prayer, suspended on the cross, pallid in death, " free among the dead" (Ps. lxxxvii. 6), ruling over hell, rising on the third day, exhibiting to His apostles the places of the nails as the memorials of His triumph, and lastly mounting up to the highest heavens in the sight of a multitude of the faithful. Now, which of these wonders cannot be made the subject of solid, loving, and sanctifying meditation ? And whichsoever of them I reflect upon, I am thinking of my God, and I know that in them all He is *my* God. Dearest brethren,

I have called it wisdom to " meditate on these things "
(1 Tim. iv. 15), and I have judged it prudence to
" eructate the memory of the abundant sweetness "
(Ps. cxliv. 7) which in these beautiful berries the
priestly Rod (Num. xvii.) has produced : which Mary
gathered on high and poured down abundantly upon
us. On high, I say, she gathered this honey and
above the sphere of the holy angels, for she received
the Word from the Father's very heart, according
to that which is written, " Day to Day uttereth the
Word" (Ps. xviii. 3). Now the Father undoubtedly can
be called by the name Day, since His Salvation, that is,
Jesus the Son of God, is designated " Day from Day "
(Ps. xcv. 2). Perhaps the name of Day can be given to
the Virgin also ? Most certainly ; she is in fact a most
beautiful Day, a Day of dazzling light " that cometh
forth as the morning rising, fair as the moon, bright
as the sun. " Consider, therefore, how Mary was exalted as high as the holy angels by the fulness of her
grace, and even higher than the angels by the coming
down of the Holy Spirit upon her. There is charity in
the angels ; they have purity also and humility : which
of these virtues did not shine forth resplendent in
Mary ? But this point has been already discussed and
established as well as was possible to me. Let me now
endeavour to show how she surpasses the angels.
I ask then : " To which of the angels hath it been said
at any time " (Heb. i. 5), " The Holy Ghost shall come
upon thee and the power of the Most High shall overshadow thee. And therefore also the Holy That shall
be born of thee shall be called the Son of God ? "
" Truth is sprung out of the earth " (Ps. lxxxiv. 12),
not from the angelic creation ; and " nowhere doth

He take hold of the angels, but of the seed of
Abrahom He taketh hold" (Heb. ii. 16). It is
high honour for the angels to be the ministers
of the Lord; but something far more sublime
has Mary merited — to be the Lord's Mother.
Her divine maternity, therefore, is the Virgin's
supereminent glory, and by this singular prerogative she is "made so much better than the
angels as she hath obtained a more excellent name
than they" (Heb. i. 4), the name, that is, of Mother
of God. This is the grace found by her who was
already full of grace: that to her fervent charity, her
unspotted virginity and her devout humility shoold
be united the privilege of conceiving her Lord without
human co-operation and bringing Him forth without
pain. But there is something still more: not only did
she conceive as a virgin and bring forth without
experiencing the ordinary pains of parturition, but
the Holy That was born of her is called and is in truth
the Son of God.

For the rest, most dearly beloved, let us strive
with all diligence, that the Word Who came forth
unto us from the mouth of the Father and through
the Virgin's womb shall not return to Him void (Is.
lv. 11), but through the same holy Virgin let us render
Him back "grace for grace" (John i. 16). Let us
" eructate the memory of the abundance of His sweetness" (Ps. cxliv. 7) until it shall be given us to
enjoy His presence, and let the rivers of grace return
to their origin so that they may flow down upon us
again in greater abundance (Eccles i. 7). For unless
they revert to their fountain-head they shall be dried
up; if we are found unfaithful in that which is little

we shall not deserve to receive that which is greater
(Matt. xxv. 21). Little, doubtless, is the remembrance
of God when compared to the delight of His presence,
little in comparison with the object of our desires,
although very great in comparison with our merits;
it is far less than what we long for but far more than
we deserve. Wisely, therefore, does the Spouse in the
Canticle return no little thanks even for this little.
For after saying to the Bridegroom, "Shew me, O
Thou Whom my soul loveth, where Thou feedest,
where Thou liest in the mid-day" (Cant. i. 6), and
receiving but a comparatively slight consolation instead of the immense boon she had solicited; a taste
of "the evening sacrifice" (Ps. cxl. 2) in lieu of the
mid-day feast: far from murmuring and losing heart
(as is commonly the case) she rather expresses her
gratitude and shows herself in all things more fervent
than ever. For well she knows that if she gives Him
proof of fidelity under the shadow of remembrance
she shall infallibly attain to the meridian light of
His presence. Therefore "you that are mindful of the
Lord, hold not your peace and give Him no silence"
(Is. lxii. 6, 7). As for those who enjoy not the memory
but the presence of the Lord: they do not need to
be exhorted; and the words addressed to them by
another Prophet: "Praise the Lord, O Jerusalem;
praise thy God, O Sion" (Ps. cxlvii. 1): belong rather
to congratulation than to exhortation. But such as
still "walk by faith" (2 Cor. v. 7) do require to be
admonished not to "hold their peace" or to "give
Him—their God—silence." For He, "the Lord God,
will speak, He will speak peace unto His people, and
unto His saints, and unto them that are converted

to the heart " (Ps. lxxxiv. 9). Yea, as " with the holy Thou wilt be holy, O Lord, and with the innocent man Thou wilt be innocent " (Ps. xvii. 26) : so wilt Thou listen to him that listens to Thee and wilt speak to him that speaks to Thee. For, my brethren, if you " hold your peace " you thereby " give Him silence." But hold your peace from what ? From the divine praises. Attend to the Prophet : " Hold not your peace and give Him no silence till He establish and till He put the praise of Jerusalem * upon the earth." " Joyful and decorous praise " (Ps. cxlvi. 1) is the praise of Jerusalem. Unless, forsooth, we are to suppose that the angelic citizens of Jerusalem delight in mutual compliments and, as men, deceive one another with foolish flattery (Ps. lxi. 10).

Almighty Father, may " Thy will be done on earth as it is in heaven " (Matt. vi. 10), so that " the praise of Jerusalem " may be established upon the earth. What is the case with us now ? The blessed angels in the holy city above seek not glory from their brother-angels, whereas men here below desire to be praised by their fellow-men ! What intolerable perversity ! But let it belong only to such as " have not the know-ledge of God " (1 Cor. xv. 34), to them that " have for-gotten the Lord their God" (1 Kings xii. 9). As for " you that are mindful of the Lord, hold not your peace," desist not from His praise until it has been established and made perfect on the earth. There is, indeed, a

* So the Saint interprets the phrase " laudem Jerusalem," taking the indeclinable noun " Jerusalem " to be in the genitive case. But it is more probably in apposition with " laudem," and thus it was understood by the Douay Translators who have rendered : " Give Him no silence till He establish and till He make Jerusalem a praise in the earth." The Greek is as ambiguous as the Latin —(Translator).

silence that cannot be blamed, nay, that rather merits commendation : just as there is speech also that is not good. Otherwise the Prophet would not have said, " It is good to wait with silence for the salvation of God " (Jer. Lam. iii. 26). It is laudable to restrain the tongue from boasting, from blasphemy, from murmuring and detraction. There is one that murmurs in his heart on account of the oppressiveness of his toil and " the burden of the day and the heats " (Matt. xx. 12) and finds fault with his superiors who " watch as being to render an account of his soul " (Heb. xiii. 17). Such murmuring is a loud clamour in the ears of God ; but this clamour of an obdurate soul is more certain than any silence to hush the voice of the Word, which it suffers not to be heard. There is another who, through " pusillanimity of spirit " (Ps. liv. 9) fails in hope : such failure is the most wicked word of blasphemy which " shall not be forgiven neither in this world nor in the world to come " (Matt. xii. 32). There is yet another who loves to " walk in great matters and in wonderful things above him " (Ps. cxxx. 1), saying to himself, " Our mighty hand hath done all these things " (Deut. xxxii. 27), " thinking himself to be something whereas he is nothing " (Gal. vi. 3). What can He Who " speaketh peace unto His people " (Ps. lxxxiv. 9) have to say to such a one ? For this soul has no need of Him : " I am rich," she says, " and made wealthy and have need of nothing " (Apoc. iii. 17). Now Truth Itself has said, " Woe to you that are rich, for you have your consolation " (Luke vi. 24) ; and also, " Blessed are they that mourn, for they shall be comforted " (Matt. v. 5). Therefore let us have peace within our souls from the censorious tongue, from the blasphemous tongue, and from the boastful tongue, because " it is good to wait with this threefold silence for the salvation of God." Yes, for then one can say, " Speak, Lord, for Thy servant heareth " (1 Kings iii. 10). The three tongues just mentioned speak not *to* but *against* the Lord. Hence Moses could say to the malcontents, " Your murmuring is not against us but against the Lord " (Exod. xvi. 8).

But, dearest brethren, although you must be silent from murmuring, from diffidence, and from boasting, be sure not to hold your peace altogether " and give Him no silence." Instead of boasting, speak to the Lord in self-accusation, that you may obtain forgiveness for the past. Instead of murmuring, speak to Him in thanksgiving, that you may receive more abundant grace in the present. And instead of losing heart, speak to Him in prayer, that you may obtain the gift of glory in the future. Confess, I say, your offences in the past, return thanks for present benefits, and then pray with all earnestness for the gifts of the future, so that He may not keep silent with regard to the forgiveness of your sins, the infusion of grace, and the promise of eternal glory in the life to come. " Hold not your peace and give Him no silence." Speak to Him so that He in turn may speak to you and each of you may be able to say with the Spouse in the Canticle, " My Beloved to me and I to Him " (Cant. ii. 16). A sweet voice this and a pleasant word. It certainly is not the voice of a murmurer, it is rather the voice of a turtle-dove. Ask me no longer, " how shall we sing the songs of the Lord in a strange land ? " (Ps. cxxxvi. 4). For that land has ceased to be reputed strange whereof the Bridegroom Himself says, " The voice of the turtle is heard in *our* land " (Cant. ii. 12). The Bride had heard Him say, " Catch us the little foxes that destroy the vines " (ibid. 15) ; and perhaps it was this that caused her to break out into the cry of exultation : " My Beloved to me and I to Him." This voice is in truth the voice of a turtle, which, being singularly chaste in its habits, perseveres in fidelity to its mate, whether living or dead : just as " neither death nor life " can separate His Spouse from the love of Christ (Rom. viii. 38). And see whether anything has been able to alienate this beloved Bridegroom from the Bride so dear to His Heart and cause Him to abandon her even when she sinned and forsook Him. A great gathering of clouds strove to intercept the light of heaven—for our iniquities made a division between us and our God (Is. lix. 2)—but the Sun of justice put forth His ardent influence and melted them all. For when wouldst thou, O religious soul, have come back to Him had He not remained constant in His love of thee, had He not cried after thee, " Return, return, O Sulamitess : return, return that We may behold thee " (Cant. vi. 12) ? Therefore, do thou likewise continue faithful to Him, so faithful that no affliction or labours shall evermore have power to frighten thee away.

My brother, thou must, like Jacob, wrestle with the Angel and not allow thyself to be overcome, because " the kingdom of heaven suffereth violence and the violent bear it away " (Matt. xi. 12). " My Beloved to me and I to Him "—what is this but wrestling ? He has given proof of His love for thee ; let Him now have proof of thine. The Lord thy God puts thee to

the trial in divers manners. Often He turns away
His face and declines from His servant, but not in
wrath (Ps. xxvi. 9). This belongs to thy probation;
it is no sign of reprobation. Thy Beloved has been
patient with thee; do thou in thy turn be patient
with Him : "Do manfully and wait for the Lord"
(ibid. 9). Thy sins were not able to conquer His
patience. Therefore let not His chastisements conquer
thine and so shalt thou obtain a blessing. But when ?
At the dawn, when "the day breaks and the shadows
retire" (Cant. ii. 17), when He has "established the
praise of Jerusalem on the earth" "Behold," so we
read, "a man wrestled with him (Jacob) till morning"
(Gen. xxxii. 24). O Lord, "cause me to hear Thy
mercy in the morning, for in Thee have I hoped"
(Ps. cxlii. 8). I will not hold my peace nor will I
give Thee any silence until the break of dawn. Would
I might also say that I will give Thee no fast ! For
Thou dost condescend even so far as to feed, but only
"among the lilies." "My Beloved to me," says the
Spouse, "and I to Him Who feedeth among the lilies"
(Cant. ii. 16). This fits in very well with what we find
earlier in the same Canticle, where, if you remember,
the first appearance of the flowers is said to synchronise
with the first sound of the turtle's voice (ibid. 12).
Yet notice that the Spouse does not inform us *what* her
Beloved feeds on, but only indicates the *place* of His
feeding ; she tells us *where* He eats His food without
explaining *what* the food is. Perhaps we are to suppose
that He finds His refreshment not so much in the
actual eating of the lilies as in being amongst them :
that He loves to be surrounded with lilies, even though
He does not make them His food. For lilies please

us rather by their odour than by their taste and they are more capable of satisfying the eye than the appetite.*

The Beloved, therefore, " feedeth among the lilies till the day break," and to the loveliness of the flowers there succeeds the richness of the fruits. For the present life is the season for flowers rather than for fruits, since we have to be satisfied with hope without possession ; and whilst " we walk by faith and not by sight " (2 Cor. v. 7) our joy comes more from the expectation than from the actual fruition of good. Consider, I pray you, the fragility of these flowers, and recollect the Apostle's admonition : " We have this treasure in earthen vessels " (2 Cor. iv. 7). Oh, how many dangers do we not see threatening the flowers of virtue ! How easily they can be punctured by the points of the thorns that surround them ! Not without cause, therefore, does the Beloved sing : "As the lily among the thorns, so is My love among the daughters " (Cant. ii. 2). Surely a " lily among the thorns " was the soul that said, " With them that hated peace I was peaceful " (Ps. cxix. 7). But " although the just man springeth forth as the lily " (Ps. xci. 13 ; Osee xiv. 6), not where there is but one lily will the Bridegroom deign to feed, for He takes no delight in singularity. Listen to what He says Himself, He Who makes His home among the lilies : " Where there are two or three gathered together in My name, there am I in the midst of them " (Matt. xviii. 20). Mark : " in the midst." Jesus always loves the middle place ; the Son of man, the " Mediator of God and men " (1 Tim. ii. 5) shows a constant dislike for holes and

* Cf. Sermons LXX.-LXXI. on the Canticle of Canticles.

corners.* "My Beloved to me and I to Him Who feedeth among the lilies." Dearest brethren, let us take care to have our souls adorned with lilies; let us hasten to root out the " thorns and thistles " (Gen. iii. 18) and to plant lilies in their place; perchance then the Beloved will sometime show Himself so condescending as to come to feed even in us.

Needless to say, He was wont to feed in Mary, and that the more abundantly in proportion to the multitude of lilies He found in her. What but a lily was the splendour of her virginity? What but lilies the glory of her humility and the supereminence of her charity? Yet we also, my brethren, can possess lilies, although of a far inferior kind. But even amongst these the Bridegroom will not disdain to feed: if yet the cheerfulness of our devotion beautifies those acts of thanksgiving whereof I have already spoken, if purity of intention brightens our prayer, if our con-

---

* It is interesting to note how often and how variously Jesus is assigned the middle place. As the Second Person of the Divinity, He occupies the middle place between the Father and the Holy Ghost; as the Logos, the uncreated Image of God (Col. i. 15), He can be said to mediate between God and the visible creation; and He is the one appointed Mediator between God and man. He was born at midnight, He was laid in the manger in the midst of the animals—" expavi in medio duorum animalium " as the Church sings in her Christmas office—He was found " sitting in the midst of the doctors " (Luke ii. 46), He " wrought salvation in the midst of the earth " (Ps. lxxiii. 12), He promised that where two or three are gathered together in His name He will be in the midst of them (Matt. xviii. 20), He stood in the midst of the people that knew Him not (John i. 26), He passed through the midst of his enemies (Luke iv. 30), "They crucified Him and with Him two others, one on each side and Jesus in the midst " (John xix. 18), after the resurrection He is often described as appearing in the midst of the disciples (Luke xxiv. 36 ; John xx. 19, 26), St. Paul represents Him as being in the midst of the church (Heb. ii. 12), and John saw Him in the midst of the golden candlesticks (Apoc. i. 13, ii. 1) and of the throne (v. 6, vii. 17) —(Translator).

fession is rendered white, so to speak, by the grace of forgiveness ; according to that which is written : " If your sins be as scarlet, they shall be made as white as snow, and if they be red as crimson they shall be white as wool" (Is. i. 18).

But, my brother, whatsoever thou hast a mind to offer to the Lord be sure to entrust it to Mary, so that thy gift shall return to the Giver of all grace through the same channel by which thou didst obtain it. God of course had the power, if He so pleased, to communicate His grace without the interposition of this Aqueduct. But he wanted to provide us with a needful intermediary. For perhaps " thy hands are full of blood " (Is. i. 15) or dirtied with bribes : perhaps thou hast not like the Prophet " shaken them free from all gifts " (Is. xxxiii. 15). Consequently, unless thou wouldst have thy gift rejected, be careful to commit to Mary the little thou desirest to offer, that the Lord may receive it through her hands, so dear to Him and most " worthy of all acceptation " (1 Tim. i. 15). For Mary's hands are the very whitest of lilies ; and assuredly the Divine Lover of lilies will never complain of anything presented by His Mother's hands that is not found among the lilies. Amen.

Hail, Mary, Full of Grace!
Grant me Thy grace most merciful Jesus, that it may
be with me and may labor with me and
continue with me to the end.

VI

ON THE FAITH AND VIRTUES OF THE BLESSED VIRGIN

" Wisdom hath built herself a house, she hath hewn her out seven pillars "—Prov. ix. 1.

" Wisdom hath built herself a house." First of all, my brethren, it is necessary to enquire what is the wisdom spoken of here. For there is more than one kind of wisdom. We have heard of the wisdom of the flesh which is " the enemy of God " (Rom. viii. 7). We have heard also of the wisdom of this world which is " foolishness before God " (1 Cor. iii. 19). Both of these are, in the words of the Apostle James, " earthly, sensual, devilish " (James iii. 15). According to wisdom in either of these senses a man is called wise when he is skilled to do evil and knows not how to do good (Jer. iv. 22). And in this his wisdom, he merits reproof and meets destruction, as it is written : " I will catch the wise in their own craftiness " (1 Cor. iii. 19), " I will destroy the wisdom of the wise, and the prudence of the prudent I will reject " (1 Cor. i. 19). It seems to me that we may, without untruth or impropriety, apply to those endowed with this kind of wisdom the words of King Solomon : " There is an evil that I have seen under the sun : a man who is wise in his own conceit." Now all such wisdom, whether of the flesh or of the world, is obviously quite incapable of building anything solid, nay, it will rather destroy every house where it is permitted to dwell. There is, however, another kind of wisdom " that is from

above," and " first indeed is chaste, then peaceable "
(James iii. 17). This, my brethren, is none other than
Christ Himself, " the Power of God and the Wisdom
of God " (1 Cor. i. 24), Who, as the Apostle further
testifies, " is made for us of God wisdom, and justice,
and sanctification, and redemption " (ibid. 30).

This Divine Wisdom, then, Who was with God and
was Himself God (John i. 1), coming down to us from the
bosom of the Father, " hath built Himself a house,"
that is, hath fashioned for Himself a Mother, the
glorious Virgin Mary, and in that most holy house He
" hath hewn out seven pillars." Now, what means
the expression, " He hath hewn out in His house seven
pillars," except that He hath prepared His Mother
by faith and good works to be a dwelling-place worthy
of His Majesty ? For three added to four make seven.
Now, the number three belongs to faith because of the
Blessed Trinity, the principal object and mystery of
faith ; whilst the number four is consecrated to good
works on account of the four-fold cardinal virtues.
I say, then, that the Three Persons of the august
Trinity dwelt in the holy Virgin by the presence of
Their undivided Majesty, although the Son alone was
in her by the assumption of human nature. So much
is clear from the words of the heavenly envoy, who,
in revealing to Mary the profound depths of this mystery,
said to her, " Hail, full of grace, the Lord is with thee "
(Luke i. 28). And a little further on : " The Holy
Ghost shall come upon thee and the Power of the Most
High shall overshadow thee " (ibid. 35). Behold now
O most happy Virgin, thou hast the Lord, thou hast
the Power of the Most High, thou hast the Holy
Ghost. Thou hast consequently the Three Divine

Persons, the Father, the Son,* and the Holy Spirit. For the Father cannot be without the Son, or the Son without the Father, or without Both the Holy Spirit Who proceeds from Both. Hence the Son once said to His disciples, "Do you not believe that I am in the Father and the Father in Me?" (John xiv. 10). And again, "The Father Who abideth in Me, He doth the works" (ibid.). It is manifest, therefore, that faith in the Trinity was found in the Virgin's heart, since it is by faith that God dwelleth in the hearts of the just (Eph. iii. 17).

Was she also endowed with the four cardinal virtues? This is a question that seems well worthy of our consideration. In the first place, then, let us see if she possessed fortitude. But how could that virtue have been wanting to one who, renouncing the pomps of the world and the pleasures of the flesh, was determined to live to God alone in the holy state of virginity? Unless I mistake, it is of this admirable Virgin King Solomon speaks when he says, "Who shall find the valiant woman? Far and from the uttermost coasts is the price of her" (Prov. xxxi. 10). So great indeed was her fortitude that she crushed the head of the "old serpent" (Apoc. xii. 9), as the Lord had predicted: "I will put enmities between thee and the woman, and thy seed and her seed: she shall crush thy head" (Gen. iii. 15). That she was temperate, prudent, and just is as clear as the daylight from the words addressed to her by the Archangel, and from her own words in reply. For when Gabriel saluted her with such extraordinary marks of respect, saying, "Hail, full of grace, the Lord is with thee," far from exulting at the thought that she was

* Christ is called the Power of God (1 Cor. i, 24).

favoured with such singular graces and privileges, she remained silent and " was troubled, and thought with herself what manner of salutation this might be " (Luke i. 29). Does she not appear in all this a most beautiful model of temperance ? And does she not give us an equally noble example of prudence when, on being informed by the Angel of the heavenly mysteries about to be accomplished in her, she made careful enquiries as to the manner of her conception and parturition, because, as she said, she knew not man (Luke i. 34) ? She practised justice * in the highest degree when she acknowledged that she was but the handmaid of the Lord (ibid. 38). For such confession is characteristic of the just, as the Prophet testifies where he says, speaking to the Lord, " But as for the just, they shall confess to Thy name, and the upright shall dwell with Thy countenance." (Ps. cxxxix. 14). And in another place we find this instruction for the just : " You shall say in your confession : all the works of the Lord are exceeding good " (Eccles. xxxix. 20 21).

Accordingly, my brethren, the Virgin Mary is a model of fortitude in her purpose to remain unmarried, of temperance in her silence under praise, of prudence in her inquiries, of justice in her confession. And it was with these four pillars of the moral virtues, added to the three others of faith—of which I have already spoken—that the Divine Wisdom built for Himself a

---

* According to St. Bernard, humility is a part of justice, whereby we give God what is due to Him and attribute to ourselves that which alone is ours—sin and nothingness : just as pride may be viewed as opposed to justice, since it consists in the appropriation by the creature of what belongs to God. Moralists, however, look upon humility as a subordinate part of the virtue of temperance. Cf. Hickey, *Ethica*, p. 117 — (Translator).

house within her ; and He so filled her mind that from the fulness thereof her very flesh was fertilised, and by an unique and wonderful privilege of grace the Virgin brought forth, clothed in flesh, the same Wisdom she had first conceived in her spotlessly pure spirit. As for ourselves, dearest brethren, if we also desire to become the house of uncreated Wisdom, it is necessary that we should be propped up with these same seven pillars, that is, we must be prepared to receive Him with faith and good works. With regard to the moral virtues, I am of opinion that justice alone will suffice us, on condition, however, that it embraces in itself the other three.* Therefore, lest it be deceived by ignorance or error, it must have prudence for guide ; and let temperance walk at its right hand and fortitude at its left, for otherwise it will be liable to slip and fall by bending unduly to one side or the other.

---

* How the perfection of Justice includes the other three cardinal virtues is explained in the *Treatise on Consideration*, ch. viii.

VII

FIRST SERMON FOR THE FEAST OF THE ANNUNCIATION

" Mercy and truth have met each other, justice and peace have kissed."—Ps. lxxxiv. 11.

" That glory may dwell in our land, mercy and truth have met each other, justice and peace have kissed." " Our glory," says the great Apostle, " is this, the testimony of our conscience " (2 Cor. ii. 12). Not such testimony as the proud Pharisee obtained, for although his deceived and deceiving conscience gave testimony to him, we know that testimony was not true (Luke xviii. 11, 12, John xix. 35) ; but the testimony which " the Spirit Himself giveth to our spirit " (Rom. viii. 16)—it is in this testimony we place our glory. Now it seems to me that this divine testimony consists in three convictions. For we ought to believe, in the first place, that we cannot obtain the pardon of our sins otherwise than through the mercy of God ; secondly, that we are powerless to do any good work whatever except by His grace ; thirdly, that by no works of ours can we merit eternal life, unless it is His good pleasure to bestow upon us this also as a free gift.* " Who can make him clean that is conceived

* But how can we be said to merit what is bestowed upon us as a free gift ? In Chapter xiii of the Saint's classic work on Grace and Free Will, we find the explanation : That which is a gift as the fruit of God's free grace is merited by our co-operation with grace ; eternal life is truly given as a reward, because it crowns our merits ; nevertheless, it is also a gratuitous gift because the merits which it crowns are themselves the fruits of God's antecedent grace : " Merita tua si bona sunt Dei dona sunt," says St. Augustine —(Translator).

110

of unclean seed " save only Him Who alone is clean ?
(Job xiv. 4). Undoubtedly, that which has been done
can never be undone : yet if God wills not to impute
it, it shall be as if it had not been. The Prophet had
this in mind when he exclaimed, " Blessed is the man
to whom the Lord hath not imputed sin " (Ps. xxxi. 2).
With regard to good works, it is absolutely certain
that no one can perform them of himself. For if human
nature was unable to stand, even whilst still in its
integrity, how much less shall it be able, corrupted as
it now is, to rise from its fall ? It is manifest that all
things tend of themselves to return to their origin,
and are always more easily moved in that direction.
So it is even with us. From nothingness we have
been created, and you know, my brethren, that if left
to ourselves we are constantly tending to sin, that is
to say, to nothingness.*

Now, as to eternal life, we know " that the sufferings
of this time are not worthy to be compared with the
glory to come " (Rom. viii. 18), no, not even if one
man were to endure them all. For human merits are

---

* That is to say, the radical reason of our proneness to sin
is found in our origin from nothingness. Compare this with
the following from Father Rickaby : " I suggest that a world
clear of all evil is an intrinsic impossibility and that the reason
why God never made such a world is that it is not makable. . . .
I am led to conjecture the intrinsic necessity of evil ' patrolling,'
as Plato says, ' all mortal nature and this region of earth '
not from any speculation on the nature and attributes of God
but from the consideration of the abyss of nothingness out of
which every creature is drawn. This kinship with nothingness
clings to all creatures. The creature cannot put off the traces
of its origin, and it is twofold. Inasmuch as it comes of God
it has whatever of goodness and positive being there is in it.
But inasmuch as it is drawn out of nothingness there attaches
to it from the first a certain defectibility, a proneness to decay
and failure—in fact, to evil " (*Oxford and Cambridge Con-
ferences*, p. 139) —(Translator).

not of such great worth as that therefore God is
obliged in strict justice to reward them with eternal
life, so that He would do us a wrong if He refused to
bestow it.* Leaving aside the fact that all our merits
are themselves only the gifts of God, so that even on
their account man is more indebted to God than God
to man : what, I ask, is all that man can merit in comparison with the glory of paradise, immense and eternal ?
Where shall we find a holier man than the Royal
Prophet, to whom the Lord Himself rendered such excellent testimony, when He said, " I have found David,
a man according to My own heart " (Acts xiii. 22) ?
Nevertheless, even he was obliged to say to God,
" Enter not into judgment with Thy servant " (Ps.
cxlii. 2). Therefore, " Let no man deceive himself "
(1 Cor. iii. 18), for if one only takes the trouble to
examine the matter as he ought he shall certainly
find that not even " with ten thousand will he be able

* This seems at first sight to clash with the definition of the
Council of Trent, Sess. 6, c. 16, can. 32 : " If anyone says that
the good works of a justified man are the gifts of God in such
a sense that they are not also the merits of the justified man
himself ; or that the justified man, by the good works he per-
forms through the grace of God and the merits of Jesus Christ
of Whom he is a living member, does not truly merit an increase
of grace, life eternal, and the actual attainment of life eternal
—provided he dies in the grace of God—and even an increase
of glory, let him be anathema." But the contradiction is only
apparent. The Saint is speaking of our merits, viz., our good
works, considered apart from God's free acceptance and promise
of reward. Now, in the view of perhaps the majority of theo-
logians such acceptance and promise are essential for the con-
dign meritoriousness of even our supernatural good works proceeding from grace " God is made our debtor," writes St.
Augustine, " not by receiving anything from us, but by His
own promise. We say to a man : thou art in my debt because
thou hast obtained of me ; but to God : Thou art in my debt
because Thou hast given me a promise. Thus, therefore, we
can demand our due from Him, saying : ' Render what Thou
hast promised, for we have done what Thou hast enjoined ' "
(Sermon 158) —(Translator).

to meet Him That with twenty thousand cometh against him " (Luke xiv. 31).

But, my brethren, these truths of which I have just been speaking are by no means sufficient : they ought rather to be considered as the beginning and, as it were, the foundation of faith. If, then, thou believest that thy sins can be blotted out by Him alone against Whom alone thou hast offended (Ps. l. 6) and to Whom alone sin has no access, " thou dost well " (James ii. 19) : but advance a step further and believe this likewise, that He has in effect forgiven thee thy transgressions. Such is the testimony which the Holy Spirit renders in thy heart, saying, " Thy sins are forgiven thee " (Matt. ix. 5). And so St. Paul " accounts a man to be justified freely by faith " (Rom. iii. 28). With respect to merits also, it is not enough to believe that they cannot be acquired except through the grace of God, unless the Spirit of truth testifies to thee that thou hast thus actually acquired them. Similarly, as regards eternal life, thou must have the testimony of the Spirit that thou shalt certainly attain to it by the divine assistance. For it is the Spirit Himself Who pardons our sins, it is He Who gives us our merits, and it is He also Who renders to us the reward of our merits.

My brethren, these " testimonies are become exceedingly credible " (Ps. xcii. 5). In the first place, I have in the Lord's passion the most conclusive evidence as to the pardon of my sins. For the voice of His Blood, Which has far greater force than that of the blood of Abel (Heb. xii. 24), proclaims aloud in the hearts of the elect the remission of all their offences. " He was delivered up for our sins," says the Apostle

(Rom. iv. 25), and we cannot doubt that His death has been more powerful and efficacious unto good for us than our sins have been unto evil. Next, as to good works, I possess an equally strong proof in the fact of the Lord's resurrection, for " He rose again for our justification " (ibid.). And concerning the hope of reward, I have the testimony of His ascension, because He ascended for our glorification (John xiv. 2). We find reference in the psalms to this threefold effect of divine mercy. In one place the Prophet sings, " Blessed is the man to whom the Lord hath not imputed sin " (Ps. xxxi. 2), in another, " Blessed is the man whose help is from Thee " (Ps. lxxxiii. 6), and elsewhere, " Blessed is the man whom Thou hast chosen and taken to Thee : he shall dwell in Thy courts " (Ps. lxiv. 5). Here, my brethren, you have true glory, a glory that dwells within us, because it is a glory given by Him Who " dwelleth by faith in our hearts " (Ephes. iii. 17). But the children of Adam, " seeking glory one from another," had no desire for " the glory which is from God alone " (John v. 44). And thus, pursuing the glory which comes from without, they possessed glory indeed, yet not so much in themselves as in the mouths of others.

Do you desire me to tell you, brethren, whence man has this indwelling glory ? I will endeavour to satisfy you in a few words, because I am anxious to proceed without further delay to a discussion of the mystical sense of my text. For it was this alone I purposed to investigate carefully in the words of the Prophet ; but that apostolic utterance regarding internal glory and the testimony of conscience suggested itself at once to my mind and turned my thoughts to the con-

sideration of the moral sense.* I say, then, that this
indwelling glory is found even here on this earth of
ours wherever "mercy and truth have met each other,
and justice and peace have kissed." For it is necessary
that the preventing mercy of God be met by the truth
of our confession and that thenceforth we should
"follow peace and holiness, that is, justice, without
which no man shall see God" (Heb. xii. 14). When a
man begins to feel compunction for his sins, that is
an effect of the divine mercy by which he is already
prevented. But it does not enter his heart until it is
met by the truth of his confession. "I have sinned
against the Lord," said David to the Prophet Nathan,
when rebuked by the latter for his double crime of
adultery and homicide. And the Prophet replied,
"The Lord also hath taken away thy sin" (2 Kings
xii. 13). Yes, because "mercy and truth had now met
each other." So much is necessary that we may
"decline from evil" (Ps. xxxvi. 27), but to "do
good" (ibid.) we must "praise the Lord in timbrel
and in choir" (Ps. cl. 4), that is to say, we must have

---

* With St. Bernard, the moral sense of a Scriptural text
signifies the practical rules of conduct derivable therefrom,
whilst the mystical sense has reference to hidden truths of the
speculative order. The more common way is to distinguish
first between the literal sense which belongs immediately to
the inspired words, and the mystical sense which is derived
mediately from the words, immediately from the actions or
objects signified by the words. The latter is then subdivided
into the allegorical sense, which deals with what we must believe,
the analogical, which concerns the objects of our hope, and the
tropological or moral, which reveals to us our duties, and so
has reference to charity, since "charity is the fulfilling of the
law" (Rom. xiii. 10). All this is found neatly expressed in the
distich :

"Litera gesta docet, quid credas allegoria,
   Moralis quid agas, quo tendas anagogia."
                                        —(Translator.)

unity and concord in bodily mortifications, in the
fruits of penance, and in the works of justice—for
" unity of spirit " (Ephes. iv. 3) is " the bond of perfection " (Col. iii. 14)—and must not turn aside either
to the right hand or to the left. For there are some
whose " right hand is the right hand of iniquity "
(Ps. cxliii. 8). Such was that proud Pharisee of whom I
have made mention, and who boasted that he was not
as the rest of men : but, as before remarked, " he gave
testimony of himself, so his testimony is not true "
(John viii. 13). But securely may he glory in whom-
soever " mercy and truth have met each other and
justice and peace have kissed " : only let him glory
not in himself but in the " Spirit of truth " (John
xiv. 17) Who renders testimony to him (2 Cor. x. 17).

" That glory may dwell in our land, mercy and truth
have met each other, justice and peace have kissed."
My brethren, if " a wise son is the glory of his father "
(Prov. x. 1), since no one can be wiser than the Son
of God, Who is Wisdom Itself, it evidently follows that
the glory of the Eternal Father is Christ, the Power of
God and the Wisdom of God " (1 Cor. i. 24). Therefore, inasmuch as " at sundry times and in divers
manners " (Heb. i. 1) it was predicted of Him by the
prophets that He would be seen upon earth and would
converse with men (Bar. iii. 38) : the Psalmist indicates
in these words how that has been fulfilled, and how,
all things being accomplished which were foretold
of Him in the Scriptures, " Glory has dwelt in our
land." It is as if he said in clear terms : " In order
that the Word might be made flesh and dwell among
us (John i. 14) mercy and truth have met each other,
justice and peace have kissed." We have come, my

brethren, to a most profound mystery, a mystery
worthy to be investigated with all diligence ; but,
alas ! we have neither minds powerful enough to fathom
it, nor, given a true understanding thereof, have we
words capable of communicating our thought. However, I will offer you my own humble sentiments, such
as they are, in the hope that they may at least " give
an occasion to a wise man " (Prov. ix. 9). It seems
to me, then, most dearly beloved, that I behold the
first man, fresh from the hand of his Creator, adorned
in particular with four virtues and, in the words of the
Prophet, " clothed with the garments of salvation "
(Is. lxi. 10). For in these four the whole of salvation
consists nor can it be had without the united presence
of them all : especially as they cease to be virtues if
they are separated from each other. The first man,
therefore, received from God the virtue of mercy as a
guardian and attendant which should at once go before
and follow after him, watch over and protect him everywhere. You perceive what kind of foster-parent the
Lord found for His little one, what a valet He provided
for newly-created man. But man, as being a noble
and rational creature, had also need of a tutor, to the
end that he might not be cared simply as a brute beast,
but brought up as a well-beloved child. Now for this
office no better master could be found than truth
itself, which would sometime lead its pupil to a knowledge of the Supreme Truth. But, in the meantime,
lest he should be found " wise to do evils " (Jer.
iv. 22) and as " knowing to do good and not doing it,
it should be sin to him " (James iv. 17), he was given
justice to guide his steps. Furthermore, he received
from the hand of his most beneficent Creator the addi-

tional endowment of peace for his solace and delight,
a twofold peace, preventing both " combats within and
fears without "* (2 Cor. vii. 5), so that neither the
flesh could " lust against the spirit " (Gal. v. 17) nor
could any external creature inspire him with alarm.
For we are told that it was Adam who as their lord
imposed what names he pleased upon all the animals
Gen. ii. 19), and even the serpent itself did not dare
to attack him with violence, but had recourse to
cunning instead. What, then, was wanting to him
who had mercy to guard him, truth to instruct him,
justice to guide him, peace to console him ?

But, alas ! this creature so highly favoured " went
down from Jerusalem to Jericho " (Luke x. 30), " unto
his folly " (Ps. xxi. 3) and utter ruin. For he " fell
among robbers " (ibid.) by whom, as we are told, he
was first of all stripped of his clothes. Is it not manifest
that he had been stripped indeed who at the coming
of the Lord complained of his nakedness (Gen. iii. 10) ?
Neither could he be reclothed nor recover the garments
of which he had been despoiled except on condition
that Christ lost His own garments. For just as he was
not able to regain the spiritual life of his soul save
through the corporal death of Christ, in the same way
he could not recover the garments taken from him
until Christ was stripped of His own. And consider
if it be not on account of these four virtues which
made up, as its four parts, the mystical vesture lost
by the first and old Adam, that the vesture of the
second and new Adam was also divided into four parts
(John xix. 23). Perhaps you desire me to tell you now

---

* " Intus pugnae, foris timores " : whereas the Apostle writes :
" foris pugnae, intus timores."

what in the Old Adam was typified by the "seamless
coat" (ibid.) of the New, which was not divided but
disposed of by lot? I am of opinion that it was the
divine image : for this is nothing sewed on, but is
rather implanted and impressed on our very nature,
and is incapable of being either parted or rent. Man
was made to God's image and likeness (Gen. i. 26),
to the image of God in his powers of understanding
and free-choice, to the likeness of God in his endowment of virtues. The likeness was lost by sin, " nevertheless man continueth as an image " (Ps. xxxviii. 7).
For not even the fire of hell shall be able to consume,
although it shall certainly cauterise this image ; it shall
burn yet not efface it. The image, therefore, is not
divided but has its destiny decided by lot. And wherever the lot of the soul may be cast, there shall the
image be too. The same is not true of the likeness :
this abides in the good, but when the soul becomes
guilty of sin, she at once undergoes a miserable change,
losing her resemblance to her Creator and " made like
to the senseless beasts " (Ps. xlviii. 13).*

But as I have stated that man was despoiled of all
his four virtues, it will be well to explain in what
manner he was despoiled of each. Justice was lost
to him when Eve hearkened to the serpent's voice and
Adam to Eve's rather than to the voice of God. There
was still, however, one resource left to them which they
might have availed of ; and the Lord Himself suggested
it to them by the examination He put them through.
But they refused to take advantage of it, rather " inclining their hearts to evil words, to make excuses in

---

* On this subject, cf. Sermons LXXX., LXXXI., LXXXII.,
on the Canticle of Canticles.

sins " (Ps. xl. 4).   For it is the first requirement of
justice that we should abstain from sin, and the second
that we should atone for sin committed by adequate
penance.   Mercy, also was lost by both our first parents :
by Eve, when she began to burn with so fierce a fire of
concupiscence that she spared neither herself, nor her
husband, nor her offspring to be, but doomed all alike
to the chastisement of a terrible curse and inevitable
death ; and by Adam, when he exposed to the divine
anger the woman for whose sake he had sinned, as if
hoping to escape the arrow of justice by hiding behind
her back.   " The woman saw that the tree was good
to eat, and fair to the eyes, and delightful to behold "
(Gen. iii. 6) ; besides, she was told by the serpent that
by eating they, to wit, she and her husband, should be
as gods (ibid. 5).   Here we have a threefold cord of
curiosity, pleasure, and vanity : and " a threefold cord
is not easily broken " (Eccles. iv. 12).   Such things alone
the world has to offer : " the concupiscence of the
flesh, and the concupiscence of the eyes, and the pride
of life " (1 John ii. 16).   It was by these our cruel
mother was " drawn away and allured " (James i. 14)
so as to renounce every instinct of mercy.   Thus also
Adam, who had felt for the woman such a vicious compassion as to be willing to sin with her, refused her
afterwards such a virtuous compassion as to be willing
to endure the penalty for her.

The woman again was despoiled of truth, first by
culpably distorting the divine words of warning, " Thou
shalt die the death " (Gen. ii. 17) to this, " Lest *perhaps*
we die " (Gen. iii. 3) ; secondly by giving credit to the
serpent, which flatly contradicted what she had been
told by God, saying, " No, you shall not die the death "

(ibid. 4). Adam, in his turn, was also despoiled of truth when he was ashamed to confess it, and resorted to the shelter of sewed fig-leaves, that is, to the covert of vain excuses. For Truth has said, " He that shall be ashamed of Me before men, I will also be ashamed of him before My Father Who is in heaven " (Luke ix. 26, Matt. x. 33). Peace, finally, was lost, because " there is no peace to the wicked, saith the Lord " (Is. xlviii. 22). For is it not manifest that they who began now to blush for their nakedness had found, like St. Paul, " an opposing law in their members " (Rom. vii. 23) ? " I was afraid," said Adam, " because I was naked " (Gen. iii. 10). Thou hadst no such fear, O wretched one, thou hadst no such fear heretofore ; neither didst thou require any sewed fig-leaves, although thy body was as naked then as it is now.

It was then—to pursue the parable of the Prophet, who represents Mercy and Truth as meeting each other and Justice and Peace as embracing—it was then, I say, that there appears to have arisen a violent contention between these virtues. For whereas Justice and Truth began to punish miserable man, Peace and Mercy, not having so much zeal for the law as their sister virtues, judged that he ought rather to be spared : as you know, the latter two virtues are bound together in a specially intimate relation, as are also indeed the two former. Hence it happened that, as the one pair continued to wreak vengeance and to scourge the unfortunate transgressor on every side, adding to present afflictions the threat of future chastisement ; the other withdrew into the heart of the Heavenly Father, " returning to God Who gave them " (Eccles. xii. 7). For He alone was thinking " thoughts of peace " (Jer.

xxix. 11) when all beside seemed to be full of affliction.
Peace gave Him no rest and Mercy "gave Him no
silence" (Is. lxii. 7), but with their pious murmurs
they both kept knocking at His heart of a Father,
whispering, "Will God then cast off for ever? Or
will He never be more favourable again? Or will God
forget to shew mercy? Or will He in anger shut up
His mercies?" (Ps. lxxvi. 8-10). And although the
"Father of mercies" (2 Cor. i. 3) seemed to dissemble
for long, in order to satisfy the zeal of Justice and Truth,
not in vain nevertheless was the importunity of the
supplicants, for their prayer was heard "in a seasonable
time" (Ps. xxxi. 6).

Perhaps we may suppose their petition to have
received some such answer as follows: "How long
will you continue to importune Me thus? Know you
not that 'I am a debtor' (Rom. i. 14) to your sisters
also, whom you behold ready girded 'to execute vengeance upon the nations' (Ps. cxlix. 7)? Let them be
called, let Truth and Justice come, so that We may
consult together about this matter." The heavenly
envoys, accordingly, set out in haste; but when they
saw the misery of men and the cruel affliction under
which they groaned, as the Prophet says, "the angels
of peace wept bitterly" (Is. xxxiii. 7). For who ever
either sought or "prayed for the things that are for
peace" (Ps. cxxi. 6) more faithfully than "the angels
of peace"? Well, let us suppose that after conferring
with her sister Justice, Truth ascended on the appointed
day, ascended even to the clouds, not yet with her
native brightness fully restored, but looking still somewhat dimmed and darkened, the effect of her indignant
zeal. Then was fulfilled what we read in the Prophet:

" O Lord, Thy mercy is in heaven, and Thy truth
mounteth even to the clouds " (Ps. xxxv. 6). Between
the litigants sat " the Father of lights " (James i. 17), and
each proceeded to support her claim with the strongest
arguments she could discover. My brethren, do you
think there is anyone who deserved to witness that
debate and who would be willing to tell us all that
happened ?   Is there anyone who heard what words
were spoken and will consent at our request to repeat
them ?   But perhaps they were "unspeakable words"
(Ecclus. xxxvi. 16) " which it is not granted to man
to utter " (2 Cor. xii. 4). I will suppose, however, that
the controversy, in effect, was something like this :
" Thy rational creature," began Mercy, " is in sore
need of compassion, because he is overwhelmed with
misery and his state very pitiful. ' It is time to have
mercy on him, for the time is come ' (Ps. ci. 14), yea,
the time is already past."   To which Truth responded,
" Rather is it necessary that Thou, O Lord, shouldst
fulfil the word Thou hast spoken. It is necessary that
the whole of Adam should die, with all those contained
in him on the day when in his disobedience he tasted
the forbidden fruit."   " But wherefore, then, O my
Father," cried Mercy, " wherefore hast Thou begotten
me if I am destined to perish so soon ? For, as Truth
herself knows well, Thy mercy has died and is no more
if Thou refusest ever to show compassion." " And
who does not know," argued Truth in her turn, " that
if this transgressor escapes the sentence of death
pronounced against him, Thy truth, O Lord, will
have perished, instead of enduring for ever (Ps.
cxvi. 2) ? "

But hereupon one of the cherubim suggested that the

disputants be referred to King Solomon,* " since," as he said, " all judgment hath been given to the Son " (John v. 22). Accordingly, " Mercy and Truth met each other " in the sight of Solomon, with the same demands and arguments as I have just rehearsed for you. " I acknowledge," said Truth, " that Mercy has good zeal but I could wish it were more ' according to knowledge ' (Rom. x. 2). For why does she judge now that a rebel ought to be spared rather than her own sister ? " " But thou thyself wouldst spare neither the rebel nor thy sister," answered Mercy, " for thou burnest with such indignation against him that thou wouldst involve me in his destruction. What evil have I done to deserve this ? If thou hast any grievance against me, let me know what it is, but if thou hast not, wherefore am I so persecuted ? "

A most momentous controversy this, my brethren, and one extremely difficult to decide. Who, witnessing it, would not have cried out, " It were better for us if this man had not been born " (Matt. xxvi. 24) ? Yes, most dearly beloved, such was the impasse arrived at. It seemed impossible to find any way of satisfying the clashing claims of Mercy and Truth with regard to man. But when Truth added that any injury done to her own interests would redound upon the Judge Himself, and that it was necessary at all hazards to safeguard the honour of the Father's word, lest any circumstance should prevent the accomplishment of that word " living and effectual " (Heb. iv. 12) : " Desist, I pray thee," interposed Peace, " desist from such

---

* Solomon, whose very name signifies " the Peaceable One," is often taken as a type of Christ, the Prince of peace — Translator).

language : disputing like this is not becoming in us : there ought to be no discord amongst the virtues."

At this, the Judge, " bowing Himself down, wrote with His finger on the earth " (John viii. 6). And the words of His writing—which Peace who sat next Him read in the hearing of all—were these : " The one says : I am undone if Adam does not die ; the other : I am undone unless he obtains mercy. Therefore, let him die a blissful death and each will have her desire." All are filled with wonder at these words of wisdom and at the manner in which the dispute has been composed and decided. For it is manifest that there is no longer cause for complaint, since the demands of both litigants can now be fully satisfied. the one having an assurance that the sinner shall die, and the other that he shall obtain mercy. " But how shall this be done (Luke i. 34) ? " they asked. " Death is most cruel and bitter, death is terrible : its very name is enough to inspire one with horror. How then can there be such a thing as a blissful death ? " To which the Judge replied : " It is indeed true that ' the death of the wicked is very evil ' (Ps. xxxiii. 22), but ' the death of the saints ' can become ' precious in the sight of the Lord ' (Ps. cxv. 6). Will death not appear precious if it becomes the portal of life, the gate of glory ? " " Yes, undoubtedly," they at once agreed, " but how shall this be done ? " " Only in one way is it possible," He answered, " and that is : if someone on whom death has no claim will consent to die, out of charity. For death shall not have power to detain the innocent, but, as it is written, a hole shall be bored through the jaw of Leviathan (Job xl. 21), and the middle wall of partition shall be broken down ' (Ephes.

ii. 14), and ' the great chaos that is fixed ' (Luke xvi. 26) between life and death shall be bridged over. I mean, if charity, which is ' strong as death ' (Cant. viii. 6), yea, stronger than death, shall ' enter into the house of that strong man,' she shall ' bind ' him and ' rob him of his goods ' (Mark iii. 27), and not only that, but by her very passage she shall make a way through the depths of the sea by which the captives may pass forth to freedom.''

This verdict seemed good and right " and worthy of all acceptation " (1 Tim. i. 15). But where was to be found that innocent one who should be willing to suffer death, not from any kind of necessity, but from choice, not because he deserved to die, but because he chose to die ? Truth " went round about the earth " (Job i. 7), but her search was vain : for no man is free from stain, not even the infant that has lived one day upon the earth (Job xiv. 4, 5, juxta LXX). Mercy in her turn searched through the whole of heaven, yet found even in the angels—I do not say wickedness (Job iv. 18) —but not enough of charity. For this triumph of charity was of right reserved to Him than Whom no one could have greater charity (John xv. 13) : that He might lay down His life for His unworthy and " unprofitable servants " (Luke xvii. 10). He does not indeed call us His servants now but His friends (John xv. 15) ; that, however, is because of His unspeakable love and amazing condescension. As for ourselves, even though we had " done all the things that are commanded us," what else ought we to say but that " we are unprofitable servants " ? But who would venture to ask of Him so great a sacrifice ? Accordingly, on the appointed day, Truth and Mercy returned, both

exceedingly anxious, because they had failed to find
what they had been seeking.

Then Peace, addressing the disappointed sisters, as
it were apart, consoled them with the words : " ' You
know nothing, neither do you consider ' (John xi. 49, 50)
that ' there is none—amongst creatures—that can do
us this good turn, no, not one ' (Ps. xiii. 1).   Let Him
Who gave the counsel assist us now to carry it out."
The King understood what was insinuated and said :
" ' It repenteth Me that I have made man.' That is, the
penalty belongs to Me,* it is necesssary for Me to suffer
the penalty, to do penance for man because it is I Who
have created him."   Then He added : " ' Behold I
come' (Ps. xxxix. 8), for ' this chalice cannot pass away
but I must drink it ' (Matt. xxvi. 42).   So, summoning
Gabriel, He gave him the command : " Go, say to the
' daughter of Sion : behold thy King cometh ' (Zach.
ix. 9)."   Away sped the Archangel, and, arriving on
earth, announced the glad tidings, saying, "Adorn thy
marriage-couch, O Sion, and prepare to receive thy
King"   Before the King came Truth and Mercy,
according to what is written, " Mercy and Truth shall
go before Thy face " (Ps. lxxxviii. 15).   It belonged
to Justice to make ready the throne, as is said in the
Psalm, " Justice and judgment are the preparation of
Thy throne " (ibid.).   As for Peace, she came down in
company with the King, " that His prophets might be
found faithful " (Ecclus. xxxvi. 18), who had predicted
that there would be peace on our earth at His coming.
Hence, at the birth of the Lord the choir of angels
sang, " Peace on earth to men of good will " (Luke

---

* The Saint considers " poenitet me " as equivalent to
poena tenet me "—(Translator).

ii. 14). It was then also that Justice and Peace, hitherto, as it seemed, not a little at variance, lovingly embraced each other. For " the justice which was of the law " (Rom. x. 5)—if indeed it deserved the name of justice —was more accustomed to condemn than to caress, rather urging by fear than leading by love. Neither did it ever reconcile itself to peace as has now been done by " the justice which is of faith " (ibid. 6). For how was it that neither Abraham, nor Moses, nor the other just men of the Old Dispensation were able after death to attain to the peace of eternal beatitude, or to enter the kingdom of peace, if not because Justice and Peace had not yet embraced ? For ourselves, dearest brethren, we ought henceforth to pursue justice with more ardent zeal, since now " Justice and Peace have kissed " and have formed an alliance of ever-lasting friendship ; so that whoever bears with him from this life the testimony of Justic e shall be wel-comed by Peace with smiling face and open arms, and " in the self-same shall sleep and rest " (Ps. iv. 9). Amen.

VIII

SECOND SERMON FOR THE FEAST OF THE ANNUNCIATION

" And the Spirit of the Lord shall rest upon Him : the spirit of wisdom and of understanding, the spirit of counsel and of fortitude, the spirit of knowledge and of piety, and He shall be filled with the spirit of the fear of the Lord "—Is. xi. 2, 3.

Brethren, to-day when we are keeping the solemnity of the Lord's annunciation, the simple history of our redemption presents itself to our view as an immense plain of most pleasing aspect. The Archangel Gabriel is charged with a new embassy, the Virgin Mary reveals to the world a new virtue and is honoured by the heavenly envoy with a new form of salutation. The ancient curse pronounced upon women (Gen. iii. 16) is now cancelled, and the new Mother receives a new benediction. She who never felt the fire of concupiscence is filled with heavenly grace; so that by the power and operation of the Holy Ghost descending upon her, she, who knows not man, may conceive in her womb the Son of the Most High God. The remedy for our ruin enters us by the same channel through which was infused the serpent's poison which corrupted the whole human race. Innumerable flowers of this kind could be gathered without labour in these pleasant fields : but it is the central abyss of awful profundity that now attracts my gaze. Truly, the mystery of the Lord's incarnation is an inscrutable abyss; an unfathomable gulf of significance yawns beneath that sentence of the Evangelist, " The Word was made flesh and dwelt amongst us" (John i. 14).

129

For who is able to penetrate it? or to sound it? or to understand it? "The well is deep and I have nothing wherein to draw" (John iv. 11). But I remember that the canvas which people sometimes use to cover the mouth of the well, is wont to be moistened by the vapour exhaling from the water. Therefore, although (conscious of my infirmity) I do not dare to plunge in, I often nevertheless "stretch forth my hands to Thee, O Lord," over the mouth of this darksome deep, because "my soul is as earth without water unto Thee" (Ps. cxlii. 6). And now, dearest brethren, whatever little moisture my weak thought has been able to absorb from the vapour uprising out of this well of mystery, I will endeavour to communicate to you ungrudgingly: I will wring the cloth so as to extract from it if possible even a few drops of the celestial dew.

And first of all, I inquire the reason why it was the Son Who became incarnate rather than the Father or the Holy Ghost, since the three Divine Persons are not alone coequal in glory and majesty but in Substance are one and the same. But "who hath known the mind of the Lord? Or who hath been His counsellor?" (Rom. xi. 34). My brethren, we are face to face with a most profound mystery upon which it would be irreverent to pronounce an opinion too lightly. It appears to me, nevertheless, that the incarnation of either the Father or the Holy Ghost would necessarily involve the confusion of a plurality of sonships, since one Person would be called the Son of God and a different the Son of man. It seems also specially appropriate that that Person in particular should become a Son in time

Who was already a Son from eternity, lest otherwise
we should have ambiguity in the name. Besides, it
is the singular glory of our Virgin, it is Mary's grandest
prerogative that she has merited to have one and the
same Son in common with God the Father, which prerogative, as is evident, would be lost to her had any
other Person but the Second become incarnate. And
with regard to ourselves finally, we should not have
the same grounds for our hope of salvation and of the
inheritance from the incarnation of either the First
Person or the Third. We are confident that He Who
was the Only-Begotten, being made now " the First-
Born amongst many brethren " (Rom. viii. 27) will
admit to participate in the inheritance those whom He
has called to share in His sonship : for if brothers,
" joint-heirs also " (ibid. 17).*

As Christ Jesus, therefore, our faithful Mediator, in
an ineffable mystery united together in His own single
Person the Substance of God and that of man : so, in
the act of reconciliation, following a counsel of infinite
wisdom, did He observe perfect equity between the
Creator and the creature, assigning to each what
was due to each, honour to the Former, mercy to the
latter. For this was the most admirable manner of
effecting a reconciliation between the offended Lord
and His guilty servant : that zeal for the Lord's honour
should not be allowed to crush the servant with too
severe a chastisement, nor, on the other hand, should
that honour suffer prejudice by excessive condescension
to the sinner. Hear, then, and ponder carefully the
division made by the angels at the very birth of this
Mediator. " Glory to God in the highest," so they

* Cf. Vol. i. of this Series, p. 6, note.

sang, " and on earth peace to men of good will " (Luke
ii. 14). And furthermore, it was that He might observe
the same distinction of equity that Christ, our faithful
Conciliator, was never without the spirit of holy fear
whereby He always showed reverence and deference
to His Father, and always sought His glory, or the
spirit of piety, by which He tenderly compassionated
men. Therefore He had need also of the spirit of
knowledge, lest without it fear and piety should be
confounded in their functions. Note here that the
first sin committed by our first parents had three
authors, and that each of them lacked a different one
of the three virtues aforesaid. The three authors of
the sin were Eve, the devil, and Adam. Now it is
manifest that Eve lacked knowledge, since, as the
Apostle says, " the woman, being seduced, was in the
transgression " (1 Tim. ii. 14). The serpent indeed had
knowledge enough, for he is represented as being " more
subtle than any of the beasts of the earth " (Gen.
iii. 1) ; yet that malignant one was without piety, being
" a murderer from the beginning " (John viii. 44). As
for Adam, it may perhaps be allowed that he possessed piety, inasmuch as he was unwilling to sadden
the woman, but he certainly forsook the fear of the
Lord by hearkening to her voice rather than to His.
Would to God it were the fear of the Lord that pre-
vailed in him, just as it is significantly said of Christ
that " He shall be filled with the spirit—not of piety,
but—of the fear of the Lord " (Is. xi. 3) ! For in all
things and always the fear of the Lord should take
precedence of piety towards our neighbour, and it is
that alone which has a right to claim possession of the
whole man. It was by means of these three virtues,

therefore, fear, piety, and knowledge, that our Mediator reconciled man to God, as it was by counsel and fortitude that He delivered him from the hand of the enemy. For by counsel He deprived the devil of his ancient power over the human race, by allowing him to lay hands on the Innocent ; and by fortitude He prevented him from forcibly retaining the redeemed when, arising victorious from the dead, He raised up together with Himself the life of us all.

From that time, my brethren, " He has fed us with the bread of life and understanding, and given us the water of wholesome wisdom to drink " (Ecclus. xv. 3). For the understanding of spiritual and invisible things is the true bread of the soul, the bread that " strengtheneth man's heart " (Ps. ciii. 15), and fortifies it for every good work and every spiritual exercise. " But the carnal man who perceiveth not these things that are of the Spirit of God, for it is foolishness to him " (1 Cor. ii. 14),—let him weep and lament, saying, " My heart is withered because I forgot to eat my bread " (Ps. ci. 5). Thus, it is an evident and absolute truth that it shall profit a man nothing " if he gain the whole world and suffer the loss of his soul " (Mark viii. 36). But when could an avaricious man be brought to understand it ? Thou wouldst only lose thy labour didst thou attempt to bring it home to him. And wherefore this ? Simply because he judges it to be foolishness. Again, what is more true than that Christ's yoke is sweet ? (Matt. xi. 30). But offer this truth to a man of the world, and see if he does not think thou art reaching him a stone instead of bread (Matt. vii. 9). Nevertheless, it cannot be doubted that it is by the understanding of such interior truths the soul properly lives, and that that is her spiritual food : for " not in (material) bread alone doth man live, but in every word that proceedeth from the mouth of God " (Deut. viii. 3, Matt. iv. 4). Certain as this is, it is equally certain that until thou hast acquired a relish for truth, it cannot without much difficulty gain admission to thy soul. But when thou beginnest to feel a delight in it, it is no longer food for thee : it has become drink, and flows easily into thy mind, so that " the water of wholesome wisdom " may help to digest " the bread of understanding," which would be rather a burden than a benefit to the members of the interior man, if they suffered from the lack of this moisture.

Therefore, my brethren, of all that was required for the salvation of His people, nothing whatever was wanting to the Saviour. For He it is of Whom the Prophet Isaias foretold : " And there shall come forth a Rod out of the Root of Jesse, and a Flower shall rise up out of his root. And the spirit of the Lord shall rest upon Him : the spirit of wisdom and of understanding, the spirit of counsel and of fortitude, the spirit of knowledge and of piety, and He shall be filled with the spirit of the fear of the Lord " (Is. xi. 1-3). Note well how the Prophet said that the Flower was to rise up out of the *root*, not out of the *rod*. But, as is obvious, if the Flesh of the Infant Christ had been newly created in the Virgin's womb, and was not derived from her substance, as some have maintained, the Flower should have been represented as arising not from the *root*, but rather from the *rod*. Consequently the fact that this Flower is declared to have arisen from the root proves beyond the possibility of a doubt the common origin of the matter composing It. In remarking that the Spirit *rested* upon the Flower, the Prophet desires to insinuate that the Spirit of God found nothing to contradict Him in the Flesh of Christ. As for ourselves, the Spirit does not yet rest in us, because He is not yet completely Master of our hearts: there still "the flesh lusteth against the Spirit and the Spirit against the flesh" (Gal. v. 17). From this domestic strife may He deliver us in Whom nothing such existed, the New Man and the True Man, Who took His true and common Flesh from the common source, yet without any of the leaven of concupiscence.

IX

THIRD SERMON FOR THE FEAST OF THE ANNUNCIATION

" The law was given by Moses, grace and truth came by Jesus Christ "—John i. 17.

How rich Thou art in Thy mercy, O Lord our God! How magnificent in Thy justice! How prodigal of Thy grace! Verily, " there is none like unto Thee " (Ps. lxxxv. 8), most munificent Benefactor, most equitable Recompenser, most loving-kind Deliverer. By Thy grace Thou hast regard to the humble (Ps. cxii. 6, Luke i. 48); by Thy justice Thou judgest the innocent; by Thy mercy Thou savest even the sinful. Such thoughts, dearest brethren, are the mystical meats set before us on the table of our wealthy Host by the testimonies of the Sacred Scriptures (Prov. xxiii. 1), and to-day in greater abundance than usual, as you shall find if you " consider diligently." We owe this unwonted profusion to the circumstance that in the present year the most solemn feast of the Lord's Annunciation falls within the holy season of Lent.* To-day, then, we have heard recited for us the story of the woman taken in adultery and absolved from her sin through the mercy of the Redeemer. To-day we have seen Him, the same indulgent Redeemer, delivering the innocent Susanna from death, and filling the most

* This sermon was preached in 1150, in which year the Feast of the Annunciation fell upon the Saturday preceding the Fourth Sunday of Lent. On that day the history of Susanna is recounted in the Office, whilst the story of the adulterous woman is read in the Gospel of the Mass — (Translator).

136

blessed Virgin with singular gifts of His gratuitous grace. Here in truth is a rich banquet, where we have served up to us at the same time mercy, grace, and justice. Is not mercy rightly regarded as the food of men ? Yea, it is a most wholesome food and very efficacious as a remedy. Is not justice, again, the bread of the heart ? Undoubtedly, and a kind of bread that wonderfully " strengtheneth the heart of man " (Ps. ciii. 15), because it is so solid and nourish‧ing. Hence it is said, " Blessed are they that hunger after justice, for they shall have their fill " (Matt. v. 6). And with regard to the grace of God, may not this also be described as the food of the soul ? Oh, certainly, and a most agreeable food it is, " having in it all that is delicious and the sweetness of every taste " (Wisdom xvi. 20) : what is more, it unites in itself the properties of the preceding two, for not alone is it pleasant, but it is also nourishing and medicinal.

Let us, therefore, approach this table and let us taste somewhat of each of these dishes. " Moses in the law commanded us to stone such a one " (John viii. 5), so said sinners of a sinner, the proud Pharisees of the adulterous woman. But, O Pharisees, you were answered " according to the hardness of your heart " (Matt. xix. 8). " Jesus bowing Himself down wrote with His finger on the earth " (John viii. 6). " Lord, bow down Thy heavens and descend " (Ps. cxliii. 5). " Bowing Himself down," and inclining towards mercy —for in the Heart of Jesus is no Judaical stiffness— He " wrote with His finger—not this time on a stone, but—on the earth." And that not once only, but a second time : He wrote twice according to the number of inscribed tables given to Moses. Perhaps we may

be allowed to suppose that by the first and second
writings He impressed on the earth truth and grace,
respectively, according to the testimony of the Apostle
John, " The law was given by Moses, grace and truth
came by Jesus Christ " (John i. 17).   And consider
further whether He may not be supposed to have
read from the first table of truth His refutation of the
Pharisees : " He that is without sin among you, let
him first cast a stone at her " (John viii. 7).   A " short
word " (Rom. ix. 28) indeed, but " living and effectual
and more piercing than any two-edged sword " (Heb.
iv. 12).   For the blush of confusion that mantled their
faces and their stealthy withdrawal showed with what
power this word of the Lord had pierced the stony
hearts of the accusers, with what force their flinty
foreheads had been broken by this little stone (1 Kings
xvii. 49).   The adulterous woman deserved stoning,
indeed, but let him be forward to punish her who is
not conscious of deserving the like punishment himself :
let him presume to wreak vengeance on the guilty,
whose conscience acquits him of similar guilt.   But as
for him who cannot pretend to such innocence, his
zeal ought to begin with himself as with the object
most within reach.   Let him first pronounce and
execute sentence upon the domestic criminal.   So far
the table of truth.

But truth is not sufficient.   It has confounded the
accusers, yet without absolving the accused.   Therefore, let the Lord Jesus write again, let Him write the
table of grace ; let Him read it for us also, and let
us, dearest brethren, be attentive.   " Woman, hath no
man condemned thee ?   Who said : No man, Lord.   And
Jesus said : Neither will I condemn thee.   Go, and now

sin no more " (John viii. 10, 11).   O voice of mercy !
O words that give to our hearing the joy of salvation !
(Ps. l. 10, 14).   Lord Jesus, " cause me to hear Thy
mercy in the morning, for in Thee have I hoped "
(Ps. cxlii. 8). For it is hope alone that can move Thee
to compassion ; it is only into the vessel of faithful
confidence that Thou pourest the oil of Thy mercy.
There is indeed a perfidious confidence which merits
nothing but maledictions : it is that which we possess
when we sin in hope.   Although properly speaking it
should not be called confidence at all, but rather in-
sensibility or pernicious dissimulation. For how can
he have any real confidence who attends not to the
danger that surrounds him ?   Or how can he who feels
no fear and recognises no object of fear possess that
which is the remedy for fear ?   Confidence is a source
of consolation.   But they need no consolation " who
are glad when they have done evil, and rejoice in most
wicked things " (Prov. ii. 14).   Consequently, my
brethren, let us, like holy Job, ask the Lord to make
known to us " how many are our iniquities and sins,"
and to reveal to us " our crimes and offences " (Job
xiii. 23).   " Let us examine our ways and our works "
(Jer. xviii. 11, Lam. iii. 40), and ponder in diligent
consideration all the perils that encompass us.   Let
each one of us cry out in the midst of his fears, " I
shall go to the gates of hell " (Is. xxxviii. 10) ; so that
henceforward the mercy of God shall be our only
comfort.   For this is true and perfect hope, when a
man despairs of himself and leans with his whole weight
upon God. This, I say, is true confidence, to which
mercy is never denied, since, as the Psalmist testifies,
" The Lord taketh pleasure in them that fear Him,

and in them that hope in His mercy" (Ps. cxlvi. 11).
And surely we have good cause for fear when we consider ourselves, and equally good reason for confidence
when we turn our gaze towards God. For He is " sweet
and mild and plenteous in mercy " (Ps. lxxxv. 5),
" ready to repent of the evil " (Joel ii. 13), and " bountiful to forgive " (Is. lv. 7). Let us at least credit His
enemies who could find in Him nothing else that might
be made a ground of accusation except His readiness
to condone. " He will compassionate this sinner," they
said among themselves, " and when she is denounced to
Him He will not suffer her to be slain. He will, therefore, stand convicted of openly contravening the law
by pardoning one whom the law condemns." But, O
Pharisees, all your malicious devising has but redounded
to your own disadvantage. By fleeing from judgment
you show that you despair of your cause ; whilst the
guilty woman, having none to accuse her, can now
receive pardon without injury to the law.

But let us consider now, most dearly beloved, in
what manner the Pharisees stole away from the scene
of judgment. " They went out one by one, beginning
with the eldest " (John viii. 9). Do you not see how
the two elders go to hide themselves in the orchard of
Joakim ? They seek his wife, the virtuous Susanna.
Let us follow them, for their minds are full of evil
purpose against her. " Consent to us" (Dan. xiii. 20)
say these elders, these Pharisees, these wolves, who
only just now have been prevented from devouring
another poor sheep, albeit a wanderer from the fold.
" Consent to us and do as we desire." " O ye that are
grown old in evil days " (ibid. 52), do you now per-
suade one to commit the same crime of which you

awhile since accused another ? But this is all your justice ; you do in secret the very things which you publicly denounce in your neighbour. Therefore it was that you " went out one by one " when He Who knows all secrets struck home to your consciences so powerfully with the words, " He that is without sin among you, let him first cast a stone at her." With good reason, then, did Truth say to His disciples, " Unless your justice abound more than that of the Scribes and Pharisees, you shall not enter into the kingdom of heaven " (Matt. v. 20). " But if thou wilt not consent to us," say these elders, " we will bear witness against thee " (Dan. xiii. 21). O seed of Chanaan and not of Juda ! Moses certainly has not commanded you this in the law. Perhaps you pretend that he requires you not only to stone the adulterous but also to accuse the virtuous ? to bear false witness against the innocent as well as to hurl stones at the guilty ? But so far is this from being the case that he does not allow the false accuser any more than the adulterer to go unpunished (Deut. xix. 16-19). The truth is that " you who make your boast of the law, by transgression of the law dishonour God " (Rom. ii. 23).

" Susanna sighed and said : I am straitened on every side " (Dan. xiii. 22). Yes, because whichever way she turned she saw death confronting her : here, bodily death ; there, the death of the soul. " If I do this thing," she went on, " it is death to me, and if I do it not, I shall not escape your hands " (ibid.). So it is, O Pharisees. Neither the virtuous nor the vicious can escape your hands, neither the sinner nor the saint is secure from your accusations. You dissemble the sins you have yourselves committed when you find

sins with others ; but if you chance to meet someone
who has not been guilty of any sin, you impute to him
your own. But what course does Susanna take, " straitened on every side," as she is, and forced to choose
between death and death, that is, between corporal
and spiritual death ? " It is better for me," she says,
" to fall into your hands without doing it, than to sin
in the sight of the Lord " (ibid.). For she knew that
" it is a fearful thing to fall into the hands of the
Living God " (Heb. x. 31). Men indeed can " kill the
body, but after that have nothing more that they
can do " : not them, consequently, ought we to fear
but rather " Him Who after He hath killed, hath power
to cast both body and soul into hell " (Luke xii. 4, 5 ;
Matt. x. 28). What keeps the servants of Joakim from
coming ? Let them rush in by the postern, for there
is an uproar in the orchard, the yelping of two old
wolves and between them the bleating of a poor
frightened little sheep. But the Lord, Who has so merci-
fully snatched from their very jaws one little deserving
to be rescued, will not now suffer them to devour the
innocent. With reason, therefore, when about to be
put to death, " her heart had confidence in the Lord "
(Dan. xiii. 35) Whom hitherto she had so much feared
as to despise in comparison all human fear, Whose law
she had preferred to both life and reputation. " For
never had there been any such word said of Susanna,"
whose " parents were just " and whose " husband was
the most honourable of all the Jews " (ibid. xxvii. 3, 4).
And with good reason also was she, who hungered so
eagerly after justice that, for its sake, she had been
willing to endure corporal death and the disgrace of
her house, and to witness the inconsolable sorrow of her

friends : with good reason, I say, was she allowed to behold her unjust persecutors condemned to receive well-merited chastisement by the sentence of a righteous judge.

And for ourselves, dearest brethren, if we desire to hear from the Lord the consoling sentence, " Neither will I condemn thee," if we wish now to sin no more against Him, if we " would live godly in Christ Jesus " (2 Tim. iii. 12) : we also must " suffer persecution " (ibid.) and that without " rendering evil for evil or railing for railing " (1 Peter iii. 9).   For he who is not patient shall lose justice, that is to say, shall lose life, that is to say, shall lose his soul (Luke xxi. 19).   " Revenge to Me, and I will repay, saith the Lord " (Rom. xii. 19).   So in truth it is.   He will undoubtedly repay thy persecutors, provided only that thou leavest revenge to Him, provided thou usurpest not His right of judgment, provided thou requitest not with evil them that render evil to thee (Ps. vii. 5).   He " executeth judgment " indeed, yet only " for them that suffer wrong " (Ps. cxlv. 7) ; " He shall reprove with equity—but only—for the meek of the earth " (Is. xi. 4).   But I fear you are growing impatient that the sweetmeats are so long delayed. You should not, however, be surprised at this, because they are truly sweetmeats.   No matter how full you may be already, you will find them no burden.   Yea, even though eructating from satiety, you will nevertheless find a relish in these.

" The angel Gabriel was sent from God into a city of Galilee called Nazareth " (Luke i. 26).   Art thou surprised, my brother, to see so small a town so highly honoured as to receive an envoy, and so noble an envoy, from so great a King ? But know that in that little town is concealed an immense treasure — concealed, I say, but only concealed from men, not also from God. What is Mary but the treasury of God ? Yes, and wherever she is, there is His heart also (Matt. vi. 21). His eyes are always upon her, and He never ceases to " regard the humility of His handmaid " (Luke i. 48). It will be allowed, I suppose, that the Only-Begotten of God the Father knows heaven. And if He knows heaven, He must likewise know Nazareth. How can He help knowing His native place ? How can He help knowing His inheritance ? For He has inherited Nazareth from His Mother, as heaven from His Father : hence He testifies of Himself that He is both the Son and the Lord of David (Matt. xxii. 44, 45). " The heaven of heaven to the Lord," sings the Psalmist, " but the earth He hath given to the children of men " (Ps. cxiii. 16). The Lord Jesus, consequently, has a just title to the possession of both heaven and earth : of heaven, because He is Lord, and of earth, because He is the Son of man. And hear how, as the Son of man, He even claims the earth for His own, and yet shares it with us as the Bridegroom of our souls : " The flowers," He says, " have appeared in our land " (Cant. ii. 12). There is a particular appropriateness in the fact that His native town was called Nazareth, which signifies " a flower." For the Flower from the " root of Jesse " (Is. xi. 1) loves the flower-bearing land : He Who calls Himself " the Flower of the field and the Lily of the valleys " (Cant. ii. 1) is delighted to " feed among the lilies " (ibid. 16). Flowers are valued for three things, viz., beauty of colour, sweetness of fragrance, and the prospect of fruit : these

may be called their threefold grace. Such a flower shalt
thou, my brother, be esteemed by God, and He will
be well pleased in thee (Matt. iii. 17), if He discovers
in thee the beauty of a virtuous life, and the sweet
fragrance of a good reputation, and the hope and desire
of a future reward. For eternal life is the fruit of the
Spirit.

"Fear not, Mary, for thou hast found grace with
God" (Luke i. 30). How much grace? Full grace
and singular grace. But is it singular I ought to say
and not rather general? To be exact, it is both
singular and general, because it is full, and the more
singular in proportion as it is also general. For she
has been endowed with general grace in a singular
degree and manner. Her grace, I say, is all the more
singular for that it is at the same time general, because
by her alone amongst all has grace been found. It is
singular, because thou alone, O Mary, hast found grace
in its fulness ; and it is general, because of this "fulness
we have all received" (John i. 10). "Blessed art
thou among women, and blessed is the fruit of thy
womb" (Luke i. 42). Yes, it is no doubt in a singular
manner the fruit of thy womb, but through thee it has
come into the hearts of us all. It was thus of old, it
was thus, I say, in the case of Gedeon : the whole of
the dew was in the fleece and the whole of it on the
floor, yet it was not all in any one part of the floor
as it was all in the fleece (Judges vi. 37-40). So in
thee alone has the wealthy, yea, boundlessly rich Lord
of heaven "emptied Himself" (Phil. ii. 7), in thee
alone has the Most High humbled Himself, in thee
alone has the Immense circumscribed Himself, becoming
" a little less than the angels " (Heb. ii. 9), in thee alone,

finally, has the Son of God, Himself true God, made Himself also the Son of Man. But to what end ? To the end that we might be enriched by His poverty, exalted by His lowliness, magnified by His littleness, and that " gained to the Lord " by His incarnation, we might be made " one spirit with Him " (1 Cor. vi. 17).

But what shall I say, brethren ? Into what manner of vessel in particular does God pour His grace ? If, as already remarked, confidence has capacity to receive mercy, and patience is receptive of justice : what kind of vessel can we pronounce to be a proper receptacle for grace ? Grace is the purest of balsams and requires a vessel of the utmost solidity. Now what is purer, what more solid than humility of heart ? Rightly, therefore, does God give His grace to the humble (James iv. 6), rightly " hath He regarded the humility of His handmaid." By what right, do you ask ? Because the humble soul is occupied by no human merit, so that the fulness of divine grace can freely flow into her. But to this humility we have to mount by certain steps. For at first, whilst a man still takes delight in sin and has not yet broken off the miserable habit by the purpose to amend, his heart is rendered by its own vices altogether incapable of receiving grace ; afterwards, also, when he has resolved to reform his conduct, to renounce for ever his old habits, the sins of his past, although they appear to be in a manner pruned as the effect of this resolution, impede, nevertheless, the inflow of grace, so long as they are allowed to abide in the soul. They abide until they are washed out by confession, until by subsequent " fruits worthy of penance " (Matt. iii. 8) they are fully atoned for. But

woe to thee if to thy former sins and vices there succeeds the more pernicious vice of ingratitude ! For
what is so evidently opposed to grace ? The fervour of
our conversion is lost little by little in course of time,
our charity is gradually cooled whilst iniquity abounds
(Matt. xxiv. 12), so that having begun in the spirit we
are consummated in the flesh (Gal. iii. 3).   Hence it
is that through our lukewarmness and ingratitude we
do not any longer " know the things that are given
us from God " (1 Cor. ii. 12).   We forsake the fear of
the Lord, we give up our pious solicitude, we acquire
habits of loquacity, curiosity, jesting, yea, even of
detraction and murmuring, wasting our time in frivolity,
shirking labour and departing from discipline when we
can do so without being observed, as if, forsooth, we
thus avoided all harm to our souls.   What wonder is
it, then, that grace cannot flow into us with such and
so many obstacles in the way ?   But even if one " be
thankful," as the Apostle says, so that " the word of
Christ " and " the word of His grace may dwell in
him " (Col. iii. 15, 16 ; Acts xx. 32), if one be devout
and watchful and fervent in spirit : let him still beware
of putting his trust in his own merits, of relying upon
his own good work.   Otherwise, divine grace will not
enter his soul.   For such a soul is already full and has
no room for the gifts of God.

Consider now that Pharisee who prayed in the
temple.   He was not an extortioner, he was not unjust,
neither was he an adulterer.   Perhaps you suppose him
to have been without the fruits of penance ?   Far
from it.   He fasted twice in the week and gave tithes
of all he possessed.   You are now perhaps thinking
that he was ungrateful ?   But hear what he said : " O

God, I give Thee thanks, etc." (Luke xviii. 11, 12).
No, the obstacle to grace in him was that his heart
was not void of self-conceit, it was not emptied out,
it was not humble but rather proud and elated. For
instead of trying to discover what was yet wanting
to him (Matt. xix. 20), he exaggerated his merits : but
what appeared to him to be the fulness of merit was
in reality the inflation of pride. Therefore, he who
imagined himself to be full " went down into his house "
empty. The Publican, on the contrary, did in truth
empty himself ; and because he took care to bring his
vessel empty, he returned with a bountiful largess of
grace. Therefore, dearest brethren, if we too wish to
find grace, let us not only abstain from sin in future,
but also do worthy penance for the sins of our past,
and let us furthermore be careful to prove ourselves
devoted to God and sincerely humble. For it is upon
souls with such dispositions that the Lord delights to
look with that loving regard whereof the Wise Man
says, " The grace of God and His mercy are with His
saints, and He hath respect to His chosen " (Wisdom
iv. 15). And possibly it is because of the four evils
mentioned He calls back the soul whom He looks upon
four distinct times, saying, " Return, return, O Sulamitess : return, return, that we may behold thee " (Cant.
vi. 12), that is lest she should remain either in a sinful
habit, or in a sinful conscience, or in tepidity and the
torpor of ingratitude, or in the blindness of self-esteem.
From which fourfold danger may He in His mercy
recall and deliver us also, " Who of God is made unto
us wisdom, and justice, and sanctification, and redemption " (1 Cor. i. 30), Jesus Christ our Lord, Who
with the Father and the Holy Ghost liveth and reigneth
one God for everlasting ages of ages. Amen.

X

FIRST SERMON FOR THE FEAST OF THE PURIFICATION OF THE BLESSED VIRGIN MARY

" We have received Thy mercy, O God, in the midst of Thy temple "—Ps. xlvii. 10.

To-day, dearest brethren, the Virgin Mother brought the Lord of the temple into the temple of the Lord. Joseph also presented to the Lord, not his own, but his Lord's own beloved Son, in Whom He was well pleased (Matt. iii. 17). Simeon recognised the Just One Whom he had been expecting, and the widow Anna likewise made her profession of faith. By these four persons was thus instituted the procession of this day's festivity, which is now celebrated in every land and by every people " with the exultation of the whole earth " (Ps. xlvii. 3). Nor should we be surprised at the smallness of this first procession, because He in Whose honour it was held was as yet but a little One. Note, however, that it included no sinner : all who took part in it were just, all were holy and perfect. But, O Lord, is it only such Thou hast come to save ? Let Thy compassion grow with the growth of Thy Body. " Men and beasts Thou wilt save, O Lord, when Thou hast multiplied Thy mercy, O God ! " (Ps. xxxv. 7, 8). In the second procession, accordingly, we see multitudes going before and multitudes following after, and the Lord borne no longer by a Virgin but by an ass's colt (Matt. xxi. 7, 8). Therefore He now disdains no one, not even those who like beasts " have rotted in their filth " (Joel i. 17). He disdains not even such,

I say ; and if they are found to be covered with the apostolic garments (Matt. xxi. 7) and imbued with the apostolic teaching, if they have purity of morals and obedience and that charity which " covereth a multitude of sins " (1 Peter iv. 8), He will not now consider them unworthy to participate in the glory of His procession. What is yet more : we can even see that for ourselves also He has reserved a share in the same glory, which to-day seems to have been conferred on so very few. And what wonder that a participation in this glory should have been reserved for us who follow Him, since it was granted in anticipation to them that went before ?

Thus, holy David, king and prophet, " rejoiced that he might see this day ; he saw it and was glad " (John viii. 56). For had he not seen it, how could he have sung of it, " We have received Thy mercy, O God, in the midst of Thy temple " (Ps. xlvii. 10) ? This mercy of the Lord was received, therefore, by David, it was received by Simeon, we also have received it, " and as many as are ordained to life everlasting " (Acts xiii. 48) : for " Jesus Christ (as) yesterday (so) to-day, and the same for ever " (Heb. xiii. 8). But notice that it is in the *midst* of the temple we receive mercy, not in the angles and corners thereof, because " there is no respect of persons with God " (Col. iii. 25). The mercy of the Lord is made common to all, it is offered to all, no man is excluded from it but such as deliberately reject it. " Thy fountains (of mercy) are conveyed abroad " (Prov. v. 16), O Lord God. Nevertheless, they still belong to Thee, and strangers shall not partake thereof (ibid. 17). He that is Thine " shall not see death before he has seen the Christ of the Lord " (Luke ii. 26), so that he may be securely dismissed in peace (ibid. 29). What matter for wonder is it that he should be dismissed in peace who bears on his breast the Christ of the Lord ? For Christ is " our peace " (Ephes. ii. 14) and He " dwelleth by faith in our hearts " (Ephes. iii. 17). But as for thee, O miserable soul, that knowest not Jesus the Guide of the way, how wilt thou set out on the road to eternity ? " For some have not the knowledge of God " (1 Cor. xv. 34). How is this, brethren ? " Because the Light is come into the world, and men loved darkness rather than the Light " (John iii. 19). " And the Light shineth in darkness," says the same Evangelist in another place, " and the darkness did not comprehend it " (John i. 5). As much as to say : The waters of the fountain are conveyed into the streets, but the stranger does not partake of them ; mercy is found in the midst of the temple, yet is approached by none of those who are destined for everlasting misery. O ye wretched ones, " there is standing in the midst of you One Whom you know not " (John i. 26) ; so that dying before you have seen the Christ of the Lord, you shall not be dismissed in peace, but rather shall be snatched away by " the roaring lions, ready to devour " (Ecclus. li. 4).

" We have received Thy mercy, O God, in the midst of Thy temple." Very different, my brethren, is this shout of joyous thanksgiving from that mournful cry of a soul in sorrow, " O Lord, Thy mercy is in heaven, and Thy truth reacheth down even to the clouds " (Ps. xxxv. 6). And good cause for grief had the Psalmist when he uttered that cry. For surely you do not imagine that the mercy of God was then in the

midst of the temple and open to all whilst it remained
the exclusive possession of the heaven-sprung spirits ?
But when the Word was made " a little less than the
angels " (Ps. viii. 6), when He was made the " one
Mediator of God and men " (1 Tim. ii. 5), and, as
" the chief corner-stone " (Ephes. ii. 20), " made peace
through the Blood of His cross both as to the things
on earth and the things that are in heaven " (Col.
i. 20) : then and thereafter we might sing, " We have
received Thy mercy, O God, in the midst of Thy
temple." For we also " were by nature children of
wrath " (Ephes. ii. 3), " but now have obtained mercy "
(Rom. xi. 30). Of what wrath were we the children,
and what is the mercy we have obtained ?   We were the
children of ignorance, of languor, and of captivity, and
we have obtained wisdom, strength, and redemption.
The ignorance of the first woman, seduced by the old
serpent, had blinded us, the weakness of the first man,
" drawn away and allured by his own concupiscence "
(James i. 14), had enfeebled us, the malice of the
devil, finding us deservedly abandoned by God, had
reduced us to servitude. Consequently, we were born,
all of us, in the first place, absolutely ignorant of " the
way of the city of our habitation " (Ps. cvi. 4) ; in the
second place, weak and languid, so that even if the
way of life were known to us, we should still have
been impeded and held back by our want of vigour ;
and in the third place, in bondage to the most wicked
and cruel of tyrants, by whose heavy yoke we should
still have been miserably oppressed, though neither
knowledge nor strength had been wanting to us. Undoubtedly, a misery so great needed great mercy and
great compassion. And if " we are now saved from

(this threefold) wrath through Him " (Rom. v. 9). "Who of God is made unto us wisdom and justice and sanctification and redemption " (1 Cor. i. 30), how vigilant ought we not to be, most dearly beloved, lest if (which God forbid !) we again incurred the divine anger, our last state should be found worse than our first (Matt. xii. 45), as being " children of wrath," not now " by nature," but by our own free will.

Therefore, dearest brethren, let us lovingly embrace the mercy which " we have received in the midst of the temple," and after the example of the blessed Anna, let us never depart from the temple of God (Luke ii. 37) : " for the temple of God is holy, which you are," as says the Apostle (1 Cor. iii. 17). This mercy " is nigh to you, even in your mouths and in your hearts " (Rom. x. 8), since " Christ dwelleth by faith in your hearts." Yes, there is His temple and there is His throne, as you do not need to be informed, unless perhaps you have forgotten what is written, " The soul of the just man is the seat of wisdom."* Therefore I now exhort you with all earnestness, and I should like to exhort my dearest children again and again, yea, without ever ceasing, not to walk according to the flesh, even though living in the flesh, lest you displease God. Let us not make ourselves the friends of this world unless we desire to forfeit the friendship of God (James iv. 4). Let us " resist the devil and he will fly from us " (ibid. 7), so that we may henceforth freely " walk in the spirit " (Gal. v. 16) and live within our own hearts. " For the corruptible body is a load upon the soul," enervating and enfeebling her, " and the

---

* Cf. *Sermons on the Canticle of Canticles*, vol. i. p. 312, note (Mount Melleray Translation) —(Translator).

earthly habitation presseth down the mind that museth upon many things " (Wisdom ix. 15), so that it cannot mount up to the things of heaven.   Hence the Apostle tells us that " the wisdom of this world is foolishness with God " (1 Cor. iii. 19) ; and whosoever suffers himself to be overcome by the wicked one is condemned to be his slave (John viii. 34).   But it is in our hearts we receive the mercy of the Lord, it is in our hearts Christ dwelleth by faith, and it is in our hearts also He " speaketh peace unto His people, and unto His saints, and unto them that are converted to the heart " (Ps. lxxxiv. 9).

XI

SECOND SERMON FOR THE FEAST OF THE PURIFICATION OF THE BLESSED VIRGIN MARY

Let them sing in the ways of the Lord, for great is the glory of the Lord."—Ps. cxxxvii. 5.

All thanks to our Saviour for having so abundantly "prevented us with the blessings of sweetness" (Ps. xx. 4), by multiplying our joys in the mysteries of His infancy! It is but a few weeks ago we were celebrating the feasts of His Nativity, Circumcision, and Manifestation to the Gentiles, and lo! another of these most sweet solemnities has dawned upon us to-day, the solemnity of His Presentation in the temple. For on this day was offered to the Creator " the noble fruit of the earth " (Is. iv. 2) ; on this day the " atoning Victim " (Num. v. 8), the " Victim acceptable to God " (1 Peter ii. 5), was brought into the temple by His parents, was awaited by the holy elders, and was presented to the Lord by Mary's virginal hands. Mary and Joseph came to " offer the sacrifice of praise " (Ps. cvi. 22), the true " morning oblation " (Exod. xxix. 41), whilst Simeon and Anna received the Saviour Child into their arms. These four persons formed the procession which is commemorated to-day with joyous festivities throughout the four quarters of the earth. And inasmuch as we ourselves also, contrary to our custom on other solemnities,* are to have a festive

* One of the charges brought by Peter Abelard against St. Bernard and his brother Cistercians was that they had all but banished processions from their solemnities : " Processionum fere totam venerationem a vobis exclusistis " (Ep. v.

procession to-day, it will be well, I think, to consider with attention the manner and the order in which we shall proceed. We shall walk two and two, holding in our hands lighted candles, lighted not from ordinary fire, but from fire that has been previously consecrated in the church by the blessing of the priest. Moreover, the last shall be first and the first last (Matt. xx. 16) in our procession, and we shall " sing in the ways of the Lord, for great is the glory of the Lord " (Ps. cxxxvii. 5).   There is a special significance, my brethren, in our proceeding thus, two and two ; for it was in this order and with the purpose of commending fraternal love * and community life that Christ sent forth the seventy-two disciples, as the Evangelist informs us (Luke x. 1). They who insist on walking alone in the

ad Bernardum). It might be answered that a main point in the Cistercian reform was the retrenchment of all luxuries, even in the domain of ceremonial worship, and the adoption of an austere simplicity in everything. Besides, the sons of Citeaux, having to live by the labour of their hands, had no time for such magnificent liturgical pageants as might be witnessed at Cluny and other places : they were often even compelled, particularly during the harvest season, when the crops had to be saved and gathered in, to intermit the celebration of Mass and to recite the diurnal hours in the open fields. Cf. *Sermons on the Canticle of Canticles*, vol. ii. p. 73 (Mount Melleray Translation)—(Translator).

  * " Our Lord and Saviour, dearest brethren, admonishes us sometimes by His words, sometimes also by His actions. For His very actions are often precepts : although performed in silence, they teach us what we ought to do. Thus, He sent His disciples, two and two, to preach the Gospel, because there are two precepts of charity, namely, the love of God and the love of one's neighbour, and because, for the love of charity, there must be at least two. For, properly speaking, one cannot have charity towards oneself : love must tend outwards to deserve the name of charity. Therefore, in sending His disciples to preach, two and two, the Lord designed to insinuate that he who has no love for his neighbour should never undertake the office of preacher."—St. Gregory the Great, Hom. xvii. in Evang.—(Translator).

procession spoil the order of the procession, and become troublesome, not only to themselves but to the whole community as well. " These are they who separate themselves, sensual men, not having the Spirit " (Jude 19), nor " careful to keep the unity of the Spirit in the bond of peace " (Ephes. iv. 3). But as " it is not good for man to be alone " (Gen. ii. 18), so neither is it permitted him to appear before the Lord with empty hands (Exod. xxiii. 15). For if even those whom " no man hath hired " are rebuked for remaining idle (Matt. xx. 6), what do not they deserve who, although they have been hired, are found idle still ? For " faith without good works is dead " James ii. 26). But our good works must be done in the fervour of charity and with an ardent desire to please God, in order that we may be found with " lamps burning in our hands " (Luke xii. 35). Otherwise there is much reason to fear that He Who has said in the Gospel, " I am come to cast fire on the earth, and what will I but that it be enkindled ? " (ibid. 49), finding us lukewarm will begin to vomit us out of His mouth (Apoc. iii. 16). That fire whereof the Saviour speaks is the holy and blessed Fire Which the Father hath sanctified and sent into the world and Which we bless in the churches, according to what is written, " In the churches bless ye God the Lord " (Ps. lxvii. 27). Our adversary also—that malicious emulator of the works of God — he also, I say, has a fire of his own : the fire of carnal concupiscence, the fire of envy and ambition, which the Saviour came not to enkindle but to quench. And whosoever shall presume to " offer before the Lord this strange fire " (Levit. x. 1), even though he should have Aaron for

his father (ibid.), he "shall die in his iniquity"
(Jer. xxxi. 30).

But in addition to the common life, and the fraternal
charity, and the good works, and the holy fervour of
which I have been speaking, we require also humility, one
of the greatest and the most necessary of the virtues, in
order that "with honour we may prevent one another"
(Rom. xii. 10), and that each one may prefer to himself
even his juniors : for that is the perfection of humility
and the fulness of justice. Furthermore, since "God
loveth a cheerful giver" (2 Cor. ix. 7), and since one
of the fruits of charity is "joy in the Holy Ghost"
(Rom. xiv. 17), let us "sing" as I have said, "in
the ways of the Lord, for great is the glory of the
Lord," let us "sing to the Lord a new canticle, because
He hath done wonderful things" (Ps. xcvii. 1). But
if in all these practices of devotion any of us should
neglect to advance and to "go forward from virtue to
virtue" (Ps. lxxxiii. 8) : let such a one know that he
belongs not to the Saviour's procession, but is standing
still, or rather is going backwards. For in the way
of life not to advance is to fall back : there "a man
never continueth in the same state" (Job xiv. 11).
Now our spiritual progress—as I remember to have
told you often already—mainly consists in this : that
we never "count ourselves to have apprehended," but
that "forgetting the things that are behind and
stretching forth ourselves to those that are before"
(Phil. iii. 13), we strive unceasingly to become better,
and keep our imperfections constantly exposed to the
eyes of divine mercy.

XII

THIRD SERMON FOR THE FEAST OF THE PURIFICATION OF THE BLESSED VIRGIN MARY

" He was offered because it was His own will "—Is. liii. 7.

We celebrate to-day, my brethren, the feast of the Blessed Virgin Mary's Purification, which was accomplished forty days after the birth of her Divine Son, as prescribed in the law of Moses (Lev. xii. 2-4). For we read in the Book of Leviticus that a woman who, in the ordinary way, gives birth to a man-child, " shall be unclean seven days, and on the eighth day the infant shall be circumcised"; thereafter, intent on cleansing and purifying herself, she abstained, such was the law, from entering the sanctuary for the space of three and thirty days, at the expiration of which she should offer her child to the Lord with the gifts enjoined. But who does not perceive that the very first phrase of this law sets the Mother of Christ free from its obligation? It looks, indeed, as if Moses was about to say simply, " If a woman gives birth to a man-child she shall be unclean," but fearing to be found guilty of the crime of blasphemy against the Lord's Mother, he premised the restricting phrase, " in the ordinary way." For where was the necessity of these words unless he foresaw that Mary was to bring forth without detriment to her virginity? It is manifest, therefore, that this law was not made for the Mother of the Lord, since she did not give birth to her Son in the ordinary way, as was predicted by Jeremias when he said, " the Lord hath created a new thing upon the earth." What new thing, do you ask? "A woman shall compass a man" (Jer. xxxi. 22). Not by man's co-operation, not according to the ordinary law of human conception, shall she conceive, but remaining ever pure and undefiled she "shall compass a man," so that, in the words of another Prophet, the Lord, coming in and going out by this Eastern Gate, shall nevertheless leave it always shut (Ezech. xliv. 2).

Let us imagine, therefore, that Mary was disturbed in mind about submitting to this ordinance of Moses, and argued thus with herself: "What need have I of purification? Why should I abstain from entering the sanctuary, I, who, without the co-operation of man, have become the living temple of the Holy Spirit? Why should I not go into the temple of the Lord, who have given birth to the Lord of the temple? In this virginal conception, in this child-birth, there has been nothing impure, nothing illicit, nothing that needs to be cleansed: for the Infant Whom I have brought forth is Himself the very Fountain of all purity, and He has come into the world to 'make purgation of sins' (Heb. i. 3). What has this legal purification to purify in me, who, spotlessly pure already, have been made purer still by my immaculate parturition?"

It is true, O most blessed Virgin, it is very true that thou hast no cause, no necessity for purification. But, tell me, had thy Son any need of circumcision? Be, therefore, amongst women as an ordinary woman, because thy Child made Himself as one of the ordinary children of men. If He willed to be circumcised, surely He wills also and much more to be offered to His Father. Offer thy Son, then, O holy Virgin, present to the Lord the "blessed Fruit of thy womb" (Luke i. 42).

Offer for the reconciliation of us all the " living sacrifice, holy, pleasing unto God " (Rom. xii. 1). Certainly, God the Father will accept this new Oblation, this most precious Victim of Whom He says, " This is My beloved Son in Whom I am well pleased " (Matt. iii. 17).

But it seems to me, brethren, that this first oblation of the Infant Saviour has about it something peculiarly sweet. For now He is merely presented to the Lord, redeemed with innocent birds and carried home again immediately by His parents. The time will come, however, when He shall be offered, no longer in the temple, no longer between the arms of holy Simeon, but outside the city and between the arms of the cross. The time will come when, so far from being redeemed Himself with foreign blood, He shall redeem all other men with His own Blood : for He is the redemption that the Father " hath sent to His people " (Ps. xc. 9). That will be the " evening sacrifice," this in the temple is the " morning sacrifice " (Exod. xxix. 41, Ps. cxl. 2). The latter is the more joyous, but the former will have greater fulness, because in it the Victim shall have arrived at the fulness of His years, whereas in the other He is offered in His infancy. But of both oblations may be understood what the Prophet predicted, " He was offered because it was His own will " (Is. liii. 7). For to-day, in the temple, He was offered, not because there was any necessity requiring this, not because He was bound by the prescription of the law, but solely because He willed it. And with regard to the sacrifice of the cross also, it was not for His deserts He was offered thereon, or because He was unable to resist the power of the Jews, but because such was

His own will. Therefore " I will voluntarily sacrifice to Thee, O God" (Ps. liii. 8), because Thou wast voluntarily offered for my salvation, and not through any necessity of Thine own.

But, dearest brethren, what have we to offer ? Or " what shall we render to the Lord for all the things that He hath rendered to us ? " (Ps. cxv. 3). He offered for us the most precious victim He possessed, yea, a victim the most precious that can be conceived. Let us, therefore, do what we can, and offer Him the best that we have, which, namely, is our own selves. He sacrificed Himself for thee : who art thou that hesitatest to sacrifice thyself for Him ? Oh, who will grant me that so lofty a majesty may condescend to accept my poor oblation ! Lord, I can boast of but two miserable possessions : I mean my body and my soul. Would that I could perfectly offer them to Thee as a sacrifice of praise ! For it were better for me, it were far more glorious and advantageous, that I should be sacrificed to Thee than abandoned to myself. " My soul is troubled within myself " (Ps. xli. 7), but in Thee my spirit shall rejoice (Luke i. 47), that is, if it be truly offered to Thee. Brethren, whilst the Lord was still by His own decree destined to die, the Jews were wont to offer Him dead victims, but now : " I live, saith the Lord : I desire not the death of the wicked, but that the wicked turn from his way and live " (Ezech. xxxiii. 11). The Lord, then, desires not my death, and shall I not willingly offer Him my life ? This is a living sacrifice, holy, pleasing unto God, " an atoning sacrifice " (Exod. xxix. 33). But at the oblation of the Lord in the temple there were, so we read, three presences, and the Lord expects to find three things present also in our oblation of ourselves. The former oblation was attended by the presence of Joseph, the husband of the Lord's Mother and the reputed father of the Lord Himself, by the presence of the Virgin Mother, and by the presence of the Child Jesus, Who was Himself the Victim being offered. Accordingly, let there be in our oblation virile constancy, continence of the flesh, and humility of heart. Let there be, I say, in the will a manly purpose to persevere, in the flesh the purity of a virgin, and in the heart the simplicity and humility of a little child. Amen.

Assumpta est Maria in coelum :
gaudent Angeli, collaudantes
benedicunt Dominum (Offertor. Miss.)

XIII

FIRST SERMON FOR THE FEAST OF THE ASSUMPTION OF THE BLESSED VIRGIN

ON THE RECEPTION OF THE SON BY THE MOTHER IN THE INCARNATION AND OF THE MOTHER BY THE SON IN THE ASSUMPTION

" Now it came to pass that He entered into a certain citadel and a certain woman received Him into her house "—Luke x. 38.

To-day, dearest brethren, the glorious Virgin ascended to heaven, bringing with her, doubtless, to the inhabitants of the holy city an abundant augmentation of their ecstatic joys. For she it is the voice of whose salutation of yore caused an infant, as yet enclosed in his mother's womb, to leap from an excess of gladness (Luke i. 41). Now, if the soul of a babe unborn melted with tenderness when Mary spoke (Cant. v. 6), what, think you, must have been the exultation of those celestial spirits when they deserved to hear her voice and to see her face and to rejoice in her blissful presence ? And with regard to ourselves, most dearly beloved, how deservedly do we keep the feast of her Assumption with all solemnity ! What reasons for rejoicing, what motives for exultation have we not on this most beautiful day ! The presence of Mary illumines the entire world, so that even the holy city above has now a more dazzling splendour from the light of this virginal Lamp. With good reason, therefore, do " thanksgiving and the voice of praise " (Is. li. 3) resound to-day through the courts of heaven. But it seems that we have as much cause

for lamentation as the angels have for joy. For if
heaven overflows with gladness from Mary's presence,
does it not seem to follow that this lower world has
equal cause to grieve for her absence ? But let us
cease to complain, because we also " have not here a
lasting city, but we seek one that is to come " (Heb.
xiii. 14), the same which the blessed Mary entered
to-day. And if we are true citizens of that heavenly
Jerusalem, we ought certainly to remember it even in
our exile, even " upon the rivers of Babylon " (Ps.
cxxxvi. 1) we ought to communicate in its gladness
and to share in its joys, above all in that which to-day
with a mighty stream " maketh the city of God joyful"
(Ps. xlv. 5), so that we, even we, may catch some of
the " drops that fall upon the earth " (Ps. lxxi. 6).
Our great Queen has gone on before us, she has gone
on, I say, and has been gloriously received, so gloriously
that we, her poor servants, walk with confidence after
our Lady, crying out to her, " Draw us : we will run
after thee to the odour of thy ointments " (Cant. i. 3).
Our exiled race has sent home an Advocate, who, being
the Mother of the Judge and also the Mother of mercy,
will be sure to advance the cause of our salvation,
humbly, indeed, yet not less efficaciously.

To-day, then, most dearly beloved, this earth of ours
sends up a most beautiful gift to heaven, so that by
the kind intercourse of mutual giving and receiving the
human order and the divine, the earthly and the
heavenly, the lowest and the highest, may be bound
together in a sweet alliance of holy friendship. For
thither ascends " the high fruit of the earth" (Is. iv. 2)
and thence comes down the best gifts and the perfect
gifts (James i. 17). Therefore, " ascending on high,"

the holy Virgin, like her Divine Son, will "give gifts to men" (Ephes. iv. 8). Who can doubt it, since she shall have both the power and the good-will ? She is the Queen of heaven, she is the Queen of mercy, and she is also the Mother of the only-begotten Son of God – a title which more than anything else commends to us the greatness of her power and her loving-kindness : unless perchance there be someone who does not believe that the Son of the Most High honours His Mother, or who hesitates to believe that the very vitals of Mary "have passed into the affection" (Ps. lxxii. 7) of charity, in consequence of having been the home wherein for nine months the "Charity That is of God" (1 John iv. 7) "dwelt corporally" (Col. ii. 9).

It is for your consolation, dearest brethren, I have made these remarks, because I know how difficult it is to discover in such spiritual poverty as ours that perfect charity which "seeketh not her own" (1 Cor. xiii. 5). But without speaking at all of the many benefits resulting to ourselves from her glorification, if we love her in truth, we ought to be glad because she goes to her Son (John xiv. 28). Yes, I repeat, we ought to rejoice with her, for otherwise, which God forbid !— we should be found utterly ungrateful to the Finder of grace (Luke i. 30). We ought to rejoice with her, because to-day she is received at her entrance into the holy city by Him Who was received by her at His entrance into the citadel (*castellum*) of this world. And oh ! with how much honour is she received and wel-comed ! with what exultation ! with what glory ! There was not upon earth a worthier place than the temple of her own most blessed womb, into which Mary might receive the Son of God ; nor is there in heaven a more

honourable seat than the royal throne upon which
to-day Mary has been exalted by Mary's Son. Full of
bliss must be pronounced both receptions, viz., that of
the Son by the Mother and that of the Mother by the
Son, and ineffable both, because both inconceivable.
For why do we read to-day throughout the whole
Church of Christ that Gospel lesson which tells how a
woman, blessed among women, received the Saviour
into her house ? * (Luke x. 38-42).   In my opinion,
the purpose is to enable us from that reception to form
some kind of estimate of this which we are now com-
memorating, or rather to help us to such a realisation
as is possible of the inestimable glory of the second
by comparison with the inestimable glory of the first.
Who indeed, even though he could " speak with the
tongues of men and of angels " (1 Cor. xiii. 1), is com-
petent to explain how, by the descent of the Holy
Ghost and the overshadowing of the Father's power
(Luke i. 35), " the Word was made Flesh " (John i. 14),
the Word by Whom all things were made (ibid. 3) ?
how the Lord of Majesty, Whom the whole created
universe cannot contain (2 Par. vi. 18) was enclosed,
made man, within the Virgin's womb ?

And who is able even to conceive with what splendour
the glorious Queen of the universe mounted heaven-
wards to-day ; with what mighty ardour of ten-
derest affection the whole multitude of the heavenly
legions issued forth to meet her and to escort her to
the seat of glory ; with what serenity of countenance,
with what loving looks, with what joyous embraces she

* The holy preacher is taking here, in an accommodated
sense, Luke x. 38, as the Church does also by appointing this
Gospel to be read on the Feast of the Assumption —(Translator).

was welcomed by her Son and lifted high above every creature to that eminence of honour which becomes so great a Mother and is worthy of so great a Son ! Happy, doubtless, were the kisses which the Mother received from the lips of her suckling Babe whilst she fondled Him on her virginal lap. But ought we not to regard as still happier those which He gives her to-day in loving salutation from His seat at the Father's right hand, when she advances to the throne of Majesty, singing her epithalamium and saying, with the Spouse in the Canticle, " Let Him kiss me with the kiss of His mouth " (Cant. i. 1) ? " Who shall declare the generation " (Is. liii. 8) of Christ ? Who shall declare the Assumption of Mary ? For the glory wherewith she is crowned in heaven is as singular as the grace she found upon earth was incomparable. If "eye hath not seen nor ear heard, nor hath it entered into the heart of man what things God hath prepared for them that love Him " (1 Cor. ii. 9) : who can say or conceive what He hath prepared for her that bore Him and that loves Him—which no one doubts—with a love unparalleled ? Oh, happy in truth is Mary and doubly happy in that she has both received the Saviour and has been received by the Saviour. In both these signal honours the dignity of the Virgin Mother appears to us equally admirable, in both the condescension of the Divine Majesty appears equally worthy of praise.

" Now it came to pass," says the Evangelist, " that He, namely, Jesus, entered into a certain citadel and a certain woman received Him into her house."

But let us break off here and occupy ourselves rather with singing the praises of God, for this is a feast which ought to be celebrated, not so much with sermons or pious exhortations, as with uninterrupted canticles of joy and thanksgiving. But inasmuch as the Gospel text just quoted contains abundance of matter for another discourse, to-morrow we shall again assemble here, and I shall communicate to you ungrudgingly whatsoever lights may be vouchsafed to me thereupon ; so that whilst we occupy our minds with the thought of so great a Virgin, the feeling of devotion may be awakened within us and we may receive the grace to correct what is defective in our conduct and to begin a better life, unto the praise and glory of Mary's Son, our Lord Jesus Christ, Who is over all things, God blessed for ever. Amen.

XIV

SECOND SERMON FOR THE FEAST OF THE ASSUMPTION

How the Spiritual House has to be swept and garnished for the Reception of Christ

" Now it came to pass that He entered into a certain citadel and a certain woman named Martha received Him into her house. And she had a sister named Mary, who sitting also at the Lord's feet heard His word. But Martha was busy about much serving "—Luke x. 38-40.

" Now it came to pass that He entered into a certain citadel and a certain woman named Martha received Him into her house " (Luke x. 38). It appears to me that I cannot do better than to subjoin to this the exclamation of the Prophet : " O Israel, how great is the house of God, and how vast is the place of His possession ! " (Bar. iii. 24). Vast beyond a doubt must that place be, in comparison with which this most spacious earth of ours is called a citadel. Do you not agree, brethren, that that land must be very vast, that country inconceivably great, since the Saviour, issuing forth therefrom and coming down to this lower world, is said to enter into a citadel ? Or does anyone doubt that the citadel of which the Evangelist makes mention is nothing else but the court of " the strong man armed " (Luke xi. 21), " the prince of this world " (John xiv. 30), upon whom a Stronger came and robbed him of his goods (Mark iii. 27) ? Dearest brethren, let us hasten to enter into that spacious abode of beatitude where there is room enough for all and no man presses on another, so that we " may be able to comprehend with all the saints what is the breadth and length and height and depth " (Eph. iii. 18) of the city of God, the heavenly Jerusalem.   There is no reason why we should despair of being admitted into that celestial city, since the King thereof, Who is also its Creator, has not disdained to come into this narrow citadel of our earthly home.

But why do I say that He entered into the citadel ? He condescended to do much more : He even entered the close prison of a Virgin's womb.   For so the Evangelist says : " A certain woman received Him into her house."   O happy woman, who was found worthy to receive not the spies sent to Jericho (Josue ii. 1), but the most mighty Despoiler of that fool who indeed " is changed as the moon " (Ecclus. xxvii. 12) ; not the emissaries of " Jesus the son of Nave " (Ecclus. xlvi. 1), but the true Jesus Himself, the Son of God. Happy, I say, is the woman whose house at the coming of the Saviour, was found " swept and garnished " indeed, but by no means " empty " (Matt. xxii. 44). For how can she be called empty whom the Archangel saluted as " full of grace " (Luke i. 22) ?   And not only that, but he also declared that the Holy Ghost was to come upon her (ibid. 35).   To what purpose, think you, if it be not to fill her to overflowing ?   To what purpose, I repeat, except that, being filled in herself by His first coming, she might be made to superabound and overflow unto us by His second ? Would to God those spiritual spices, those precious gifts of grace were poured out upon us, so that of so great a fulness we might all receive ! (John i. 16).   For Mary is our Mediatrix ; she it is through whom " we have received Thy mercy, O God " (Ps. xlvii. 10) ;

she it is through whom we have received the Lord
Jesus into our houses. My brethren, we have each
of us his own house and each of us his own citadel.
Divine Wisdom knocks at our several doors; " if any
man shall hear His voice and open to Him the door,
He will come into him and will sup with him "
(Apoc. iii. 20). It is a common saying, one that is
often enough in the mouths of men, but more often
still in their hearts : He that takes good care of his
body guards a noble citadel. But such is not the
language of the Wise Man ; he rather counsels : " With
all watchfulness keep thy heart, because life issueth
out from it " (Prov. iv. 23).

Let us yield this point, however, and let us say
with the multitude : He that takes good care of his
body, guards a noble citadel. But it remains to be
asked : in what way are we to guard this noble citadel ?
Does it seem to you, my brethren, that that soul
has guarded the citadel of her body as she ought, whose
members she has suffered to conspire, so to speak, and
to hand over to the enemy the possession thereof ?
For there are some who " have entered into a league
with death and have made a covenant with hell"
(Is. xxviii. 15). " The beloved one," says Moses, " grew
fat and kicked, he grew fat and thick and gross "
(Deut. xxxii. 15). Such, doubtless, is the manner of
guarding the body which is praised by the sinner in
the desires of his flesh (Ps. x. 111, juxta Heb.). What
think you, brethren ? Ought we to yield to the
multitude in this matter as well ? God forbid ! Let
us rather interrogate Paul, that most strenuous leader
in the spiritual combat. Tell us, then, O blessed Apostle,
how thou guardest the citadel of thy body. " I so

run," he says, "not as at an uncertainty ; I so fight, not as one beating the air. For I chastise my body and bring it into subjection, lest perhaps, when I have preached to others, I myself should become a castaway " (1 Cor. ix. 26, 27). And in another place he writes, " Let not sin reign in your mortal body, so as to obey the lusts thereof " (Rom. vi. 12). This beyond doubt is a useful custody, and happy the soul that thus guards her body so that the enemy may never claim it for his own. There was a time when the wicked one had subjected this citadel of mine to his tyrannic sway, ruling its members with the authority of a master.* Its present desolation and misery bear witness still to the severity of its sufferings during that period. Alas ! there is left in it neither the wall of continence nor the bulwark of patience (Jer. Lam. ii. 8). The cruel oppressor " hath laid waste the vineyard " (Ps. lxxix. 14), cut down the corn, and rooted up the fruit trees. At his instigation, even " mine eye hath wasted my soul " (Jer. Lam. iii. 51), so that " unless the Lord had been my helper, my soul had almost dwelt in hell " (Ps. xciii. 17) : I speak of the " lower hell " (Ps. lxxxv. 13) where no one shall confess to Him (Ps. vi. 6) and out of which there is no deliverance.

But even as it was, my soul was not without a hell and a prison-house. For having been made captive at the very beginning of this detestable conspiracy and betrayal, she was confined and guarded as a prisoner

---

* This and what follows must not be taken literally, but only as one of those pious exaggerations to which the saints are often prone. St. Bernard, according to all his biographers, lived a most innocent life from the cradle and probably never lost his baptismal innocence —(Translator).

in her own house, whilst the jailers assigned to her
were none other than the members of her household.
Her conscience became her prison, and her torturers
her reason and her memory, cruel torturers indeed,
harsh and pitiless, but far less terrible than the lions
" roaring, ready to devour " (Ecclus. li. 4) to which
she was on the point of being abandoned. " Blessed
be the Lord Who hath not given me to be a prey to
their teeth " (Ps. cxxiii. 6). Yes, " blessed be the
Lord God of Israel because He hath visited and wrought
the redemption " (Luke i. 68) of my soul. For whilst
the malignant one was preparing to thrust her down into
the "lower hell " and designing to burn the citadel itself
with everlasting flames, so that the bodily members also
should be punished as their perfidy deserved : there
appeared upon the scene a Mightier than he. Jesus
" entered into the citadel," and " first binding the
strong man, robbed him of his goods " (Mark iii. 27),
so that He might " make unto honour " the vessels
that were " unto dishonour " (Rom. ix. 21). " He
hath broken the gates of brass and burst the iron
bars " (Ps. cvi. 16), and " brought forth the captive
out of prison " (Is. lii. 7) and out of the shadow of
death " (Ps. cvi. 10). Now it is only through confession such a captive can be delivered. Confession is
the broom, so to speak, by means of which the prison-
house puts off its forbidding aspect and reassumes its
former home-like appearance, being first " swept, and
garnished " (Matt. xii. 44) afterwards with the beautiful
green rushes of regular observances. The woman has
now a home, she has now a place for the entertain-
ment of Him to Whom she is so deeply indebted by
reason of countless favours bestowed. Woe to her if

she refuses to receive Him, if she neglects to detain Him, if she does not constrain Him to stay with her, " because it is towards evening " (Luke xxiv. 29) For he that has been driven forth shall find on his return the house " swept and garnished " indeed, but without an occupant. Then shall he go and, taking with him seven other spirits worse than himself, entering in he shall dwell there (Matt. xii. 45).

Thus, dearest brethren, her house is " left desolate " (Matt. xxiii. 38) to the soul that neglects to make it worthy of the Saviour's presence. But you may desire to know how this can be. Is it possible, you may feel inclined to ask, that a house " swept " by confession of past sins and " garnished " with regular observance should nevertheless be reputed unworthy to be inhabited by heavenly grace or to be entered by the Saviour ? Most certainly, my brethren, it is possible, if only the exterior parts of the house have been swept clean and adorned, as I have said, with the green rushes of faithful discipline, whilst all within is covered with filth. Surely no one believes that the Lord can be worthily entertained in the " whited sepulchres " of the dead, " which outwardly appear to men beautiful but within are full of all filthiness " (Matt. xxiii. 27) and corruption. I allow that occasionally, allured as it were by the attractive appearance of the outside, He begins to enter, and has already, so to speak, one foot on the threshold, by the bestowal of some first grace of divine visitation : but does He not immediately withdraw in anger ? Does He not at once take flight, exclaiming "I have stuck fast in the mire of the deep and there is here nothing solid " (Ps. lxviii 3). That is, there is no true and solid virtue but only an appearance, a quality as it were without a substance. But the thin varnish of an externally virtuous life affords no firm footing for the entrance of Christ, Who penetrates all things and desires to make His dwelling in the very centre of the heart. We are told that the Spirit of discipline " will not dwell in a body manifestly subject to sins " (Wisdom i. 4) ; but He will not alone avoid, He will flee and remove Himself far from the body where sins lie concealed, covered with the simulation of virtue. What else is that but a detestable simulation, if, instead of plucking up vice by the roots within, we content ourselves with pruning it on the exterior ? Oh, be sure it will sprout again more abundantly than before ; be sure the malicious tenant that has been expelled will come back again " with seven other spirits more wicked than himself " (Matt. xii. 45) and re-enter the house, " finding it swept and garnished " indeed, yet " empty." For " the dog that returneth to his vomit " (Prov. xxvi. 11) becomes more hateful than ever ; and he is made " a child of hell " (Matt. xxiii. 15) many times worse than before, whosoever, after obtaining the pardon of his sins, falls back into the same, like " the sow that was washed wallowing again in the mire " (2 Peter ii. 20).

Brethren, do you wish to behold a house that is " swept and garnished " but " empty " ? Look at that man who has confessed and renounced " sins manifest, going before to judgment " (1 Tim. v. 24), and who now applies nothing but his hands to the works of justice, going through every spiritual exercise with a heart devoid of all devotion and merely from custom, as the " heifer of Ephraim, taught to love to tread out the corn " (Osee x. 11). With regard to

exterior observances which are " profitable to little "
(1 Tim. iv. 8), he passes over not " one jot or one
tittle " (Matt. v. 18), although whilst "straining out a
gnat he swallows a camel " (Matt. xxiii. 24). For in
his heart he is the slave of self-will, of avarice, of vainglory, of ambition, fostering secretly, if not all these
vices together, at least each of them in turn.   And
so " iniquity lieth to itself " (Ps. xxvi. 12), although
" God is not deceived " (Gal. vi. 7).   For you may
sometimes see a man so perfectly tricked out in the
colours of virtues as to deceive even himself, not
noticing the worm that devours his vitals. He considers everything secure because the fair exterior is
still preserved. In the words of the Prophet, " Strangers
have devoured his strength and he hath not known "
(Osee vii. 9). He says to himself, " I am rich, and
made wealthy and have need of nothing," whereas he
is " wretched and miserable, and poor " (Apoc. iii. 17).
Yes, and given the due conditions you shall see the
corrupted matter, now concealed, welling out from the
festering sore, and the tree that has been pruned but
not uprooted sending out new branches in greater
abundance than ever. Dearest brethren, if we would
avoid this danger, let us lay the axe, not to the
branches, but to the root of the trees (Matt. iii. 10).
Let there be found in us not only " bodily exercise "
which by itself " is profitable to little " (1 Tim. iv. 8),
but " piety " also, which " is profitable to all things "
(ibid.), and the practice of solid virtue.

"A certain woman," says the Evangelist, "named
Martha, received Him into her house ; and she had a
sister called Mary." Martha and Mary are sisters and
so, like good sisters, should live under the same roof.

The former is " busy with much serving," the latter
attends exclusively to the words of Christ (ibid. 39, 40).
To Martha appertains the " garnishing " of the house,
to Mary the filling thereof, so that it shall not be
found " empty " : for her time is left vacant to attend
to the Lord that the house itself may not be left vacant
by Him.   But, brethren, to whom can we assign the
sweeping ? For if we are able to discover someone for
this, the house into which the Saviour is received shall
be found " swept and garnished " in truth yet not
" empty." Suppose, then, we give the broom to Lazarus,
that is, unless you have something better to suggest.
Being a brother to the two sisters, he has a right to
share their home.   I am speaking, observe, of that
Lazarus who, after he had been four days in the tomb
and was already corrupted, was awakened from the
dead by " the voice of power " (Ps. lxvii. 34). He can
therefore be considered without the least impropriety
as the type of holy penitence. We may suppose, then,
that the Saviour will enter and visit often that house
which is swept by the penitent Lazarus, which is garnished by the busy Martha, and filled by the reposeful
Mary whilst she occupies herself with the contemplation of spiritual things.

But perchance someone, piously curious, is anxious
to know why it is that in this Gospel lesson there is
no mention at all of Lazarus ?   To my mind, this
omission is quite in accord with the mystical interpretation I have just proposed to you. For the Holy
Spirit, intending that we should understand the house
of our Gospel to be Mary's virginal soul, avoids, as is
only becoming, any allusion to penitence which pre-
supposes sin. God forbid that this house should be

said to have ever had any such defilement of its
own so as to need the broom of Lazarus !   Even
supposing that the Virgin inherited the original stain
from her parents,* Christian piety will not allow us to
believe that she was less sanctified in the womb than
was the Prophet Jeremias (Jer. i. 5) or less filled with
the Holy Ghost than the Baptist (Luke i. 44). Besides,
had she not been born holy, her birthday would not
be honoured throughout the universal Church with such
joyous festivities. Finally, since there can be no doubt
at all that Mary was cleansed from the inherited defilement by grace alone—just as it is by grace alone that
stain is now washed away in the sacrament of baptism,
whilst with the " knives of stone " (Josue v. 11) alone
it could be removed under the former Dispensation :
such being the case, and the holy Virgin being entirely
free from personal sin, as we all piously believe, it
follows that her most innocent heart could have had
no experience of penitence.   Therefore, let Lazarus
abide with them that have need to " cleanse their conscience from dead works " (Heb. ix. 14) ; let him dwell
with " the wounded sleeping in the sepulchres " (Ps.
lxxxvii. 6) : but in the Virgin's home let none be found
save the sisters Mary and Martha. For did she not
act the part of Martha whilst for three months she
humbly attended her aged cousin Elizabeth, who was
about to become a mother (Luke i. 56) ? And she fulfilled the role of Mary when she kept all the words
that were said of her Son, " pondering them in her
heart " (Luke ii. 19).

* For St. Bernard's attitude towards the doctrine of Mary's
Immaculate Conception, cf. Sermons on the Canticle of Canticles
vol. i. 253-4 ; ii. 429 and Passaglia, de Im. Conc. iii. 1820-43.

Let no one be surprised, therefore, that the woman who received the Saviour is called, not Mary, but Martha : because this incomparable Virgin is found to unite in her single self the busy ministrations of Martha and the equally busy repose of Mary. For not only is it said that "all the glory of the King's daughter is within " (Ps. xliv. 14), but likewise that she is "clothed round about with varieties, in golden borders " (ibid.). For the Virgin Mary is not one of the foolish virgins ; she is the most prudent of virgins : not only is she possessed of a lamp, but she has oil also in her vessel (Matt. xxv. 2-4). You have not forgotten, I suppose, the Gospel parable which represents the foolish virgins as excluded from the wedding-feast ? Now, their house was certainly swept, because they are said to have been virgins ; it was garnished too, since we are told that all the virgins together, that is, both the wise and the foolish, trimmed their lamps ; but it was empty, for the reason that they had no oil in their lamps. Hence it was that the Heavenly Bridegroom deigned neither to be received by them into their house nor to admit them to the marriage supper in His own. Very different from these was that " valiant woman " (Prov. xxxi. 10) by whom has been crushed the serpent's head (Gen. iii. 15). For amongst the many eulogies pronounced upon her by the Wise Man you may read this also : " Her lamp shall not be put out in the night " (Prov. xxxi. 18). This has been said as a reproach to the foolish virgins, who, when the Bridegroom came at midnight, began to lament all too late that their lamps had gone out (Matt. xxv. 8). But our glorious Virgin advanced to meet Him with her lamp alight and burning so brightly as to astonish the very angels of light (2 Cor. xi. 14), causing them to exclaim, " Who is she that cometh forth as the morning rising, fair as the moon, bright as the sun, terrible as an army set in array ? " (Cant. vi. 9). For Mary surpasses in splendour all other creatures, being anointed and filled with the oil of grace above her fellows (Ps. xliv. 8) by Him Who is the Author of grace, Jesus Christ, her Son and our Lord.

XV

THIRD SERMON FOR THE FEAST OF THE ASSUMPTION

ON THE DIFFERENT EMPLOYMENTS OF MARTHA, MARY, AND LAZARUS

" Martha, Martha, thou art careful and art troubled about many things. But one thing is necessary. Mary hath chosen the best part, which shall not be taken away from her "— Luke x. 41, 42.

Jesus " entered into a certain citadel, and a certain woman named Martha received Him into her house " (Luke x. 38). How is it, my brethren, that of the two sisters only one is said to have received the Saviour, and she the lesser of the two ? For we know from the testimony of Him Whom Martha received that " Mary hath chosen the best part " (ibid. 42). Martha, however, seems to have been the elder, and, as is obvious enough, the beginning of salvation belongs rather to action than to contemplation. Christ praises Mary, but it is Martha who receives Him. So of old Jacob loved his Rachel, but during the night her sister Lia was put in her place without his perceiving it ; and when he complained of the fraud practised upon him, he was informed that " it is not the custom to give the younger in marriage first " (Gen. xxix. 24-26). Now, if you consider that the house here in question is an earthly house, you will easily understand why it was Martha and not Mary who received the Lord into it. It was to Martha rather than to Mary the Apostle addressed himself when he said, " Glorify and bear

God in your body " (1 Cor. vi. 20). For the former employs the body as a means of well-doing, whereas to the latter it is more a hindrance than a help. This is what we read in Wisdom : " The corruptible body is a load upon the soul, and the earthly habitation presseth down the mind that museth upon many things " (Wisdom ix. 15). Yes, it " presseth down the mind that museth," but not the mind that is busy about exterior ministrations. On earth, therefore, it is Martha who receives the Saviour into her house, whilst Mary considers rather how she may be received by Him into that " house not made with hands, eternal in heaven " (2 Cor. v. 1). Perhaps, however, she also can be said to receive Him into her house, but in a spiritual sense : for the Lord is a Spirit (John iv. 24).

" And she—that is to say, Martha—had a sister named Mary, who sitting also at the Lord's feet, heard His word." You observe how the Saviour was received by both sisters, by the one in His bodily presence, by the other in His speech. " But Martha was busy about much serving. Who stood and said : Lord, hast Thou no care that my sister hath left me alone to serve ? " Brethren, are we to suppose that the sound of murmuring is heard in the house where Christ is entertained ? Oh, happy the house, blessed for ever the community in which Martha has reason to complain thus of Mary ! But, on the other hand, it would certainly be shameful and even sinful on the part of Mary to envy Martha. For where in the Gospel do we find Mary complaining of Martha and saying to the Lord, " My sister hath left me alone in the enjoyment of contemplative repose " ? God forbid it, my dearest brethren, God forbid it, I say, that he who has ample leisure for prayer should ever wish to exchange his lot for the distracted life led by such members of the community as have to busy themselves about external things ! For Martha, indeed, it would be well that she should always seem to herself insufficient and unsuited for the task assigned her and should desire to see the office she holds transferred to some other. " But the Lord answering said to her : Martha, Martha, thou art careful and art troubled about many things." See what a prerogative is Mary's ! What an apologist she has against all kinds of censors ! If the Pharisee becomes indignant (Luke vii. 39), if Martha complains, if the disciples murmur (Matt. xxvi. 8) : Mary always holds her peace and Christ takes it upon Him to defend her. " Mary hath chosen the best part," says He, " which shall not be taken away from her " for ever. This is the " one thing that is necessary " ; this is the one thing that the Prophet prayed for so earnestly, as he tells us in the psalm, " One thing I have asked of the Lord, this will I seek after " (Ps. xxvi. 4).

But, my brethren, how are we to understand these words of the Lord : " Mary hath chosen the best part " ? For if her part be the more excellent, what truth is there in the answer we are accustomed to make whenever we find her disposed to regard as iniquity the bustling solicitude of the busy Martha : " Better is the iniquity of a man than a woman doing a good turn " (Ecclus. xlii. 14) ? Or what meaning can there be in the Saviour's words : " If any man minister to Me, him will My Father honour " (John xii. 26), " Whosoever will be the greater among you, let him be your minister " (Matt. xx. 26) ? Or lastly, what comfort can it be for the toiling Martha to hear herself reproved in the

praises bestowed upon her leisured sister ?   It seems
to me, consequently, that we must adopt one or other
of two interpretations : either say that Mary is commended for choosing the contemplative life, as in itself
the better part, so that, in as far as it depends upon
us, we should all make the same choice ; or that she
is praised for her detachment, in neither refusing nor
over-eagerly embracing either part but showing herself
ready to obey in all things the will of her Lord.   For
" who is so faithful as David, going out and coming in
and proceeding in all things according to the King's
command ? " (1 Kings xxii. 14): Hence he says in one
of his psalms, " My heart is ready, O Lord, my heart
is ready " (Ps. lvi. 8), ready, that is, for either one part
or the other ; ready to enjoy Thee in peaceful contemplation or to minister to Thee in the person of my
neighbour.   Here in truth is " the best part which
shall not be taken away " ; here you have the most
excellent of dispositions, which remains always the same
no matter to which side it may happen to be sum-
moned.   " They that have ministered well," so says
the Apostle, " shall purchase to themselves a good
degree " (1 Tim. iii. 13). Perhaps they shall purchase a
still better degree whosoever shall have devoted themselves well to the prayer of God.   But the best degree
shall undoubtedly be assigned to such as shall have
attained to perfection in both the active and the contemplative lives.   There is one more remark I should
like to make here. I am not sure whether it is permis-
sible to suspect anything such of Martha, but does it
not seem to you as if she regarded as idle the sister
whom she asked to be given her as a helper ?   But
he that reproves the contemplative soul for her want

of activity is evidently one of the " sensual men " and
" perceiveth not these things that are of the Spirit of
God " (1 Cor. ii. 14).   Let him know, therefore, that
this is the best part, which is destined to endure for
ever.   But as for the soul that has never practised
divine contemplation, when she arrives there where
this is the one occupation, the one concern, the very
life of all, how can she appear otherwise than awkward,
so to speak, and out of place ?

But, dearest brethren, let us consider how rightly
ordered charity has distributed these three spiritual
employments in this house of ours, allotting to Martha
the external administration, to Mary interior contemplation, and the practice of penance to Lazarus.   It is
true, all three occupations are found united in every
perfect soul ; nevertheless, different souls seem to be
intended more particularly for different functions, some
being called to the repose of prayer, others to the
exercise of fraternal charity, others again to the practice
of penance, " recounting all their years in the bitterness of their soul " (Is. xxxviii. 15), " like the slain
sleeping in the sepulchres " (Ps. lxviii. 6).   Such a
division appears to be plainly necessary, so that Mary's
mind may be occupied with loving and lofty sentiments of her God, Martha's with kind and compassionate thoughts of her neighbour, and that the mind of
Lazarus may think of nothing but his own misery and
abjection.   Let each one consider with himself to which
of these grades he belongs.   " If these three men, Noe,
Daniel and Job, shall be found in this city : they shall
deliver their own souls by their justice, saith the Lord
of Hosts . . . but they shall deliver neither sons nor
daughters " (Ezech. xiv. 14-16).   I flatter no man.

Would to God I were equally certain that none of you flattered and deceived himself ! They to whom no office has been given, no administration entrusted, their part undoubtedly is either to sit with Mary at the feet of Jesus, or else to sit with Lazarus within the sepulchral vault. As for Martha, what wonder is it that she is " troubled about many things," since she has care of many things ? But thou that art under no obligation to submit to such distractions, oughtest either not to be troubled at all, but rather to "delight in the Lord " (Ps. xxxvi. 4), or, if that be not yet possible, thou oughtest to be troubled not " about many things," but only about one, that is, about thine own self, like the Psalmist (Ps. xli. 7).

I will repeat what has just been said, so that no one may have the excuse of ignorance : thou, my brother, who hast nothing to do with building the ark of Noe or with piloting the same through the waters of the flood, oughtest to be " a man of desires " as was Daniel (Dan. ix. 23), or like the blessed Job, " a man of sorrows and acquainted with infirmity " (Is. cliii. 3). Otherwise, I fear lest, being found luke-warm and nauseous, He should vomit thee out of His mouth, Who desires to find thee either warmed from the consideration of Himself and glowing with the heat of charity, or else humbled and cold from the one thought of thine own misery (Apoc. iii. 16), having " extinguished all the fiery darts of the most wicked one " (Ephes. vi. 16) with the water of holy compunction. But even Martha herself also needs to be admonished that this is especially " required among the dispensers, that a man be found faithful " (1 Cor. iv. 2). Now a dispenser will be faithful if he neither "seeks the things that are his own, but the things that are Jesus Christ's" (Phil. ii. 21), so that his intention may be pure ; nor does his own will, but the will of his Lord, so that his actions may be rightly ordered. For there are some whose eye is not simple (Matt. vi. 22), and such as these "have received their reward" (ibid. 2). There are others who follow the guidance of their own natural feelings in everything they do, so that whatever they offer appears tainted, their own will being found in all their oblations (Is. lviii. 3). Come with me now, dearest brethren, to the inspired nuptial song, and let us consider how the Heavenly Bridegroom, where He calls to Him His Bride, has neither omitted any of these three occupations nor added to them a fourth. "Arise," He says, "make haste, My friend, My dove, My beautiful one, and come" (Cant. ii. 10). Does she not deserve to be called His friend who, wholly intent on making profit for her Master, carries her fidelity so far as to be willing even to lay down her life for Him ? (John xv. 13). For as often as she interrupts her spiritual exercises in order to minister to one of His least brethren (Matt. xxv. 40), so often does she lay down her life, in a spiritual sense, for His sake. And is she not beautiful who, "beholding the glory of the Lord with open face, is transformed into the same image, from glory to glory, as by the Spirit of the Lord" (2 Cor. iii. 18) ? And is she not a dove who laments and sighs "in the clefts of the rock, in the hollow places of the wall" (Cant. ii. 14), as if buried beneath a sepulchral slab ?

"A certain woman named Martha received Him into her house." It admits of no doubt, dearest brethren, that Martha represents the officials of the monastery, who are charged, all in the interests of fraternal charity, with the different external administrations. And would to God I myself deserved " to be found faithful among the dispensers " (1 Cor. iv. 2) ! For to whom, I ask, are the words of the Lord : " Martha, Martha, thou art careful " : more evidently applicable than to religious superiors, provided they govern with due solicitude for the welfare of their charge ? And who is " troubled about many things," if not the superior that has to watch over Mary in her contemplative repose and over Lazarus in his exercises of penance and even over them to whose shoulders he has transferred a share of the burden of government ? Behold the " careful " Martha, behold Martha " troubled about many things," in the person of the Apostle who, whilst admonishing prelates of the solicitude required of them, was himself burdened with " solicitude for all the churches " (2 Cor. xi. 28). " Who is weak," he exclaimed, " and I am not weak ? Who is scandalised, and I am not on fire ? " (ibid. 29). Therefore, let Martha receive the Lord into her house, since to her has been entrusted the administration of the house. Martha holds the position of a mediatrix, and it is her business to obtain grace and salvation both for herself and for all committed to her care, according to what is written, " Let the mountains receive peace for the people, and the hills justice " (Ps. lxxii. 3). Let the superior's assistants exercise hospitality towards the Saviour in the manner determined by their office, some being appointed to welcome Him, others to attend Him, others to minister to Him in His members, this one in the sick brethren, that one in the poor, a third in the guests and strangers.

Whilst all these are thus " busy about much serving,"

let Mary see how she shall occupy her leisure, let her
" taste and see that the Lord is sweet " (Ps. xxxiii. 9).
Let her consider, I say, how with fervour of heart
and tranquillity of mind she may sit at the feet of
Jesus, " setting Him always in her sight " (Ps. xv. 8)
and receiving the words of grace that fall from His
mouth, Whose speech is as sweet as His countenance
is lovely. For " grace is poured abroad on His lips,"
and " He is beautiful above the sons of men " (Ps.
xliv. 3), yea, beautiful above all the glories of the
angelic choirs. Rejoice, then, O Mary, and be thankful
too for that thou hast indeed " chosen the best part."
Blessed are the eyes that see what thou seest, blessed
the ears that deserve to hear what thou hearest. Oh,
blessed in truth art thou that " receivest the veins of
the divine whisper " (Job iv. 12) in the silence wherewith " it is good for a man to await the salvation of
God " (Jer. Lam. iii. 26). Be simple with thy Lord,
putting away from thee not alone all guile and simulation, but equally all multiplicity of occupation, so
that thou mayest converse freely with Him Whose
voice is so sweet and Whose face so comely (Cant.
ii. 14). There is one thing against which thou must
be on thy guard : thou must not begin to " abound
in thine own sense " (Rom. xiv. 5) or wish " to be more
wise than it behoveth to be wise " (Rom. xii. 3), lest
perchance in pursuing the light thou shouldst fall into
darkness, led astray by " the noon-day devil " (Ps.
xc. 6), concerning whom this is not the proper time
to speak. But what has become of Lazarus ? " Where
have you laid him ? " (John xi. 34). I am addressing
the sisters who have buried their brother by their preaching and their ministration, by their example and their

prayer. Where then have you laid him ? He is " hidden in the digged earth " (Is. ii. 10), he lies beneath the stone of the sepulchre, it will not be easy to find him. It will not appear improper, therefore, if I reserve to be the subject of my fourth sermon him who " is now of four days " (John xi. 39) ; so that after the Saviour's example on hearing the announcement, " Behold he whom Thou lovest is sick," I also shall rest here for to-day.

XVI

FOURTH SERMON FOR THE FEAST OF THE ASSUMPTION

ON THE RESURRECTION OF LAZARUS AND ON THE DIGNITY AND VIRTUES OF MARY

*" When He had said these things, He cried with a loud voice :
Lazarus, come forth "*—John xi. 43.

Dearest brethren, this is a time when all flesh
should shout for joy, because the Mother of the Word
made flesh is assumed into heaven ; nor should human
mortality desist from singing songs of praise on this
glorious festival, when the nature of man is elevated
in the Virgin to solitary eminence, high above all the
orders of immortal spirits. But whilst my devotion
to God's blessed Mother will not suffer me to be silent
concerning her glories to-day, I feel persuaded, on
the other hand, that neither my barren mind can conceive nor my unpolished tongue express anything worthy
of so grand a theme. Even the very princes of the
heavenly court, contemplating so great a wonder, cannot help crying out in admiration, " Who is she that
cometh up from the desert flowing with delights ? "
(Cant. viii. 5). Which may be paraphrased as follows :
" Who is this glorious creature ? And how is it that
one coming up from the desert of earth overflows with
such delights ? For delights similar to these cannot
be found even amongst ourselves who are made joyful
in the city of God by the stream of the river (Ps.
xlv. 5), and who are made to drink of the torrent of

pleasure that flows from the vision of glory (Ps. xxxv. 9).
Who can she be that thus cometh up flowing with
spiritual delights, cometh up from under the sun where
there is nothing but labour and sorrow and affliction
of spirit ? (Eccles. i. 17)." Why may I not call by the
name of delights that splendour of virginity united to
the gift of fecundity, that loveliness of humility, that
"dropping honeycomb " of divine charity (Cant. iv. 11),
those " bowels of mercy " (Luke i. 78), that fulness of
heavenly grace, that prerogative of singular glory ?
The Queen of the universe, therefore, going up from the
desert, " is become lovely and sweet in her delights," as
the Church sings,* even to the holy angels.   Nevertheless, let them cease to wonder at the delights found
in this our desert, recollecting that, according to what
is promised in the psalm, " the Lord hath given
goodness and our earth hath yielded her fruit " (Ps.
lxxxiv. 13). For why should they wonder to see Mary
" going up flowing with delights " from the desert of
this earth ?   Surely there is more reason to wonder
at Christ coming down in poverty from the abounding
wealth of the heavenly kingdom.   For it appears to
be a far more astounding thing that the Son of God
should be " made a little less than the angels " (Ps.
viii. 6), than that the Mother of God should be exalted
above the angels. His emptying of Himself has been
the filling of us (Phil. ii. 7), His miseries are our delights.
For " being rich He became poor for our sakes, that
through His poverty we might be made rich " (2 Cor.

---

* " Speciosa facta es et suavis
    In deliciis tuis, sancta Dei Genetrix."
Versicle and responsory used at Lauds and Vespers of this
festival as also on other feasts of the Blessed Virgin —
(Translator).

viii. 9). Yea, even the shame of His cross is become
the glory of His disciples (Gal. vi. 14).

But not only did Christ, Who is our Life (Col. iii. 4),
empty Himself for our sakes, He even hastened to the
sepulchre in order to recall from the dead him that
was already " of four days " (John xi. 39) ; and He
sought Lazarus – who, if your charity remembers, is to
be according to promise the subject of the sermon
to-day— in order to be sought and to be found by
Lazarus. For " in this is charity : not as though we
had loved God, but because He hath first loved us "
(1 John iv. 10). Go, then, O Lord, seek him whom
Thou lovest so as to make him also a seeker and a
lover. Inquire where they have laid him (John xi. 34) :
for he lies concealed under the stone, bound and burdened. He lies in the prison-house of his conscience,
he is bound with the bands of discipline, he is burdened and oppressed with the heaviness of his penance
as with the weight of a superincumbent slab ; particularly because he has not yet attained to that charity
which is " strong as death" (Cant. viii. 6) and " beareth
all things " (1 Cor. xiii. 4). And in this state " he
stinketh, for he is now of four days " (John xi. 39).
I think the minds of many of you have anticipated
my words and already understand whom I am speaking of under the name of Lazarus. Anyhow, the Lazarus
I refer to is he who has just recently died to sin (Rom.
vi. 2), and has " digged in the wall " of his conscience
so that he can see the many " wicked abominations "
(Ezech. viii. 8-9) of his corrupt and inscrutable heart;
or in the words of another prophet, he has " entered
into the rock and hidden in the digged earth from the
face of the fury of the Lord " (Is. ii. 10).

But, my brethren, how are we to understand the words, " Lord, by this time he stinketh, for he is now of four days " (John xi. 39)?   For it may be this stench and these days have a deeper signification than appears on the surface.   As for me, I take the first day to be the day of holy fear, wherein, our hearts being illuminated, we die to sin and are buried, so to speak, in the sepulchre of our conscience.   The second day, so it seems to me, is passed amidst the labours of conflict.   For in the beginning of our conversion to God we are wont to be assailed with particular violence by temptations arising from evil habits and can scarcely " extinguish the fiery darts of the most wicked one " (Ephes. vi. 16).*   The third day I consider to be the day of sorrow.   For it is then one " recounts all his years in the bitterness of his soul " (Is. xxxviii. 15), and is more occupied in bewailing the sins of the past than in labouring to avoid future offences.   Are you surprised to hear me explaining the days in this sense ? But remember these are the days that belong to the sepulchre, days of darkness and clouds, of affliction and lamentation (Soph. i. 15).   There follows next the day of shame, a day not unlike the three preceding, in which the miserable soul is overwhelmed with horrible confusion, whilst she ponders on the multitude and magnitude of her crimes and sadly reviews with the eyes of the heart the repulsive images of her past

---

* Similarly in the magnificent discourse preached to the clergy of Paris and entitled "De Conversione," the holy Doctor says : " It is the lesson of our daily experience that when a man seriously resolves to amend his life, he begins at once to be more fiercely assaulted by the concupiscence of the flesh ; he is, as it were, like the Israelites of old, more cruelly oppressed in works of brick and clay for attempting to flee out of Egypt and from the power of King Pharo " (Exod. v) —(Translator).

offences.   The soul in this state hides nothing from
herself : she rather examines everything, makes much
of everything, even magnifies everything.   Far from
being over-lenient, she judges her own case with the
most rigorous severity.   But such severity is profitable,
such cruelty is found worthy of the divine compassion.
For she easily obtains the grace of God when in the
interests of His glory she exercises justice against
herself.   Nevertheless, " Lazarus, come forth " (John
xi. 43) now from the tomb and do not remain too long
in this stench of corruption ; because the flesh that is
malodorous is nigh to rottenness, and he that is ex-
cessively confounded and afflicted for his sins is not
far from the brink of despair.   Wherefore, " Lazarus,
come forth."   " Abyss calleth on abyss " (Ps. xli. 8),
the abyss of light and mercy on the abyss of misery
and darkness.   The goodness of God is greater than
thine iniquity, and where sin abounds, causes grace to
abound the more (Rom. v. 20).   " Lazarus, come forth,"
that is to say : " How long wilt thou remain under the
cloud of thy conscience ?   How long wilt thou ' be
contrite upon thy bed' (Ps. iv. 5) in heaviness of heart ?
Come forth, walk abroad, rejoice in the light and free
air of My compassion.   This is only what thou hast
read in the Prophet, ' With My praise I will bridle
thee lest thou shouldst perish ' (Is. xlviii. 9).   And more
clearly still another prophet says of himself, ' My soul
is troubled within myself, therefore will I remember
Thee ' (Ps. xli. 7)."

Now what is the mystical meaning of the Saviour's
command to " take away the stone," and a little later
to " loose him and let him go " ? (John xi. 39-44).
Are we to suppose, my brethren, that after being visited

by the grace of consolation our Lazarus will cease to
" do penance, because the kingdom of heaven is at
hand " (Matt. iii. 4), or will renounce " discipline, and
so perchance the Lord be angry and he perish from the
just way " (Ps. ii. 12) ? God forbid! No, let the stone
indeed be taken away, but let penance remain, penance
that no longer burdens and oppresses the sick soul,
but rather gives fresh life and vigour to the already
revived and vigorous soul ; for that which before she
would not touch is now become her food, namely, to
do the will of the Lord (Job vi. 7, John iv. 34). So
too with discipline which has ceased to be a restraint
upon her freedom, according to the words of the
Apostle : " The law was not made for the just man "
(1 Tim. i. 9), and serves now only to direct her willing
steps " into the ways of peace " (Luke i. 79). It is
manifestly to this spiritual resuscitation of Lazarus the
Royal Prophet is alluding when he says, speaking to
the Lord, " Thou wilt not leave my soul in hell "
(Ps. xv. 10), because, as I remember to have remarked
in the sermon for the second day of this feast, a guilty
conscience may be called the hell or the prison of the
soul. " Nor wilt Thou give Thy holy one (observe,
the Prophet does not say, " *my* holy one," but " *Thy*
holy one," viz., the one whom Thou hast made holy)
to see corruption " (ibid.) ; although he was nigh to
corruption, since he was already " of four days " and
had begun to give out an offensive odour. Yea, he
was on the point of utter dissolution and of " falling
into the depths of evils " in which " the wicked man
contemneth " (Prov. xviii. 3). But prevented by " the
voice of power " (Ps. lxvii. 34) and reanimated by the
same, he gives thanks in the words, " Thou hast made

known to me the ways of life, Thou shalt fill me with
joy with Thy countenance " (Ps. xv. 10, 11). That is
to say, " In order that she may begin to contemplate
the beauty of Thy face, ' Thou hast brought forth my
soul from hell ' (Ps. xxix. 4), where ' my spirit was
in anguish within me ' (Ps. cxlii. 4) contemplating the
exceeding loathsomeness of the face of its own conscience." " He cried," says the Evangelist, " with a
great (*magna*) voice." Justly indeed is that voice
called great, not so much because of its loudness as
by reason of its piety and its irresistible power.

But whither have we come ? Had we not begun to
follow the Virgin in her flight to the heaven of heavens ?
And behold, with Lazarus, we have descended into the
abyss ! The sermon has dropped on a sudden from
the splendour of virtue to the stench of a corpse four
days in the sepulchre ! What is the cause of this, my
brethren, unless it be that I have been borne down
by my own weight, that I have been attracted earth-
ward by the abundance of matter found here ready to
hand, and not less familiar than abundant ? I acknowledge my incapacity to discourse on lofty themes,
I make no attempt to hide my timidity. It is true,
there is nothing gives me greater delight than to preach
on the glories of the Virgin Mother, yet neither is there
anything that causes me greater fear. For without
speaking of the unutterable treasure of her merits or
of her absolutely unique prerogative as Mother of God,
she is—as indeed she well deserves—loved by all with
such tender affection, so highly honoured and vener-
ated, that although everyone is eager to glorify her
name, whatever can be said on that ineffable subject,
for the sole reason that it *can* be said, does not fully

satisfy, does not fully please, is not quite acceptable. How, in truth, could that little be other than unsatisfying, that little which the human intellect can comprehend of such incomprehensible glory? If I begin to speak in praise of her virginity, behold many other virgins after her seem to present themselves before me (Ps. xliv. 15). Should I extol her humility, perhaps again others may be found, even though but few, who have learned from her Divine Son to be "meek and humble of heart" (Matt. xi. 29). And when I wish to proclaim the multitude of her mercies, I recall that there have been some besides her remarkable for mercy both men and women. There is one thing, however, with regard to which, as the Poet sings, she

> Had no precursor in the years before
> And peerless shall remain for evermore,
> In whom with joys of motherhood we find
> The glory of virginity combined — SEDULIUS.

"Mary," said the Lord, "hath chosen the best part." Oh, truly "the best part," because although conjugal fecundity is good, and virginal chastity better, more excellent than either is virginal fecundity, or should I call it fecund virginity? This is Mary's grand prerogative: it shall not be given to any other, because it "shall not be taken away from her." It is an unique privilege and at the same time ineffable, so that to speak about it in a worthy manner is as impossible as to attain to it. But what shall we say of her when we remember Whose Mother she is? What tongue, I ask, whether angelic or human, can worthily eulogise this Virgin Mother, the Mother not of a mere man but of true God? We have here, my brethren, a double wonder, a double prerogative, a double miracle. Yet the two things combine in a glorious and most perfect harmony. For no other son save God would have been worthy of the Virgin nor would any mother but the Virgin have been worthy of God.

Yet, my brethren, if you examine diligently, you will find that not alone this union of virginity with motherhood, but likewise all the various virtues which appear to be common to many are really singular in Mary. Thus, for example, what purity can be anywhere found, even amongst the holy angels, comparable to the purity of her who was deemed worthy to be made the living sanctuary of the Holy Spirit and the dwelling of the Son of God? If we estimate the value of things from their rarity, she undoubtedly must be ranked over all who was the first amongst mortals to conceive the design of emulating upon earth the life of the angels. "How shall this be done," she asked the angel, "because I know not man?" (Luke i. 34). You see, my brethren, so firm was her purpose to live always as a virgin that it could not be shaken even by the words of the heavenly envoy promising her a son. "How shall this be done?" It cannot be in the ordinary way "because I know not man," and neither the desire of a son nor the hope of posterity shall ever induce me to abandon my resolution of remaining always a virgin.

And oh! how sublime and how precious in her was the virtue of humility, united with such transcendent purity, with such spotless innocence, with such a sinless conscience, with such a fulness of grace! Whence, O most blessed One, whence hast thou humility, and humility so great? This is the humility that deserved to be regarded by the Lord (Luke i. 48), it is the beauty of this virtue the King hath desired (Ps. xliv. 12), and it is by the sweetness of its fragrance He has been drawn down to earth from His eternal home in the bosom of the Father (John i. 18). Notice how completely in accord is the Canticle of our Virgin with the nuptial song of the Old Testament, which in truth is not surprising, since Mary's womb is the Bridegroom's marriage-bed. " He hath regarded the humility of His handmaid," so sings the Virgin in her Magnificat (Luke, ibid.) ; and hear what she says in the epithalamium, " While the King was at His repose, my spikenard sent forth the odour thereof " (Cant. i. 11). Spikenard, as you know, is a lowly herb with purgative properties. Hence we may conclude that by the name spikenard is designated humility, through the odour and beauty of which Mary " hath found grace with God " (Luke i. 30).

Let him, O most blessed Virgin, let him refuse to extol thy mercy, who—if there be any—remembers to have invoked thy assistance and to have found thee wanting to him in his hour of need. As for us, thy poor servants, we congratulate thee on thine other virtues, but on this we rather congratulate ourselves. We praise thy virginity, we admire thy humility, but, because we are so miserable, more consoling to us than either is thy mercy : we love thy mercy more tenderly, we recall it more frequently, we more often invoke it. And the reason is, because it is to thy mercy we owe the restoration of the whole world and the salvation of all. For it is manifest that thou wast solicitous for the salvation of the entire human race when it was said to thee, " Fear not, Mary, for thou hast found grace with God," the grace, that is, which thou wast

seeking. Who, then, shall be able to " comprehend
what is the breadth and length and height and depth"
(Ephes. iii. 18) of thy mercy, O Virgin most blessed ?
Its length stretches forward even as far as the day of
doom to succour all that invoke it. Its breadth is as
broad as the universe, so that of thee too it can be
said, " the whole earth is full of thy mercy" (Ps.
xxxii. 5). Its height reaches up to the city of God
the ruins whereof it has been the means of repairing.
And its depth goes down to them that " sit in darkness and in the shadow of death " (Ps. cvi. 10) for
whom it has obtained redemption. For it is through
thee, O Mary, that heaven has been filled, that hell
has been emptied, that the breaches in the wall of the
spiritual Jerusalem have been repaired (Ps. l. 20), and
that the life they had lost has been restored to
miserable, expectant mortals. Thus has thy all-power-
ful and most tender charity abounded not alone in
sentiments of compassion but also in deeds of mercy,
equally rich in both.

Therefore, my dearest brethren, let us run with
thirsting souls to this fountain of mercy, let our misery
have recourse with all the eagerness of desire to this
treasury of compassion. Behold, O most blessed One,
such are the affections with which we have striven to
accompany thee to-day on thy heavenward path to
reunion with thy Son. Henceforth, I beseech thee, let
it be the concern of thy loving-kindness to make known
to the whole world the grace thou hast found with
God, by obtaining through thy holy prayers pardon
for the guilty, health for the sick, courage for the
pusillanimous, consolation for the afflicted, help and
deliverance for all in danger. On this day also, this

day of festivity and universal rejoicing, may we, thy poor servants, O Queen most benign, who praise and invoke thy most sweet name of Mary : may we deserve to receive through thy intercession an abundant largess of His heavenly grace from Jesus Christ, thy Son and our Lord, Who is over all things, God blessed for ever. Amen.

XVII

SERMON FOR THE SUNDAY WITHIN THE OCTAVE OF THE ASSUMPTION

ON THE DIGNITY OF MARY AND ON THE MYSTICAL STARS THAT CONSTITUTE HER CROWN

" And a great sign appeared in heaven : a woman clothed with the sun, and the moon under her feet, and on her head a crown of twelve stars "—Apoc. xii. 1.

It is true, most dearly beloved, that the first man and the first woman did us grievous harm, but—thanks be to God !—by another Man and another Woman all that was lost has been restored to us, not without the addition of abundant grace. For " not as the offence, so also the gift " (Rom. v. 15) : the magnitude of the grace won for us by Christ exceeds beyond all proportion the ruin wrought by Adam. Instead of breaking that which was injured (Matt. xxii. 20), the Almighty Creator in His infinite wisdom and goodness restored it to its original perfection, yea, made it better than it had been before, forming a new Adam from the ancient and giving us in Mary a second Eve. Christ alone would no doubt have been sufficient, for even now " all our sufficiency is from Him " (2 Cor. iii. 5) ; but it was not good for us that the Man should be alone (Gen. ii. 18). It seemed more congruous that as both sexes contributed to the ruin of our race, so should both have a part in the work of reparation. A truly faithful and powerful " Mediator of God and men is the Man Christ Jesus " (1 Tim. ii. 5) ; but the Majesty of His Godhead inspires mortals with fear. His Manhood seems to be swallowed up in His Divinity, not that there is any real confusion of the Natures, but because His human affections are in a manner deified. He is the Lord to Whom we have to sing not mercy alone, but " mercy and judgment " (Ps. c. 1) : because although " He learned compassion by the things which He suffered " (Heb. v. 8) " that He might become merciful " (Heb. ii. 17), He has also to exercise the judicial office (John v. 22). It is written, moreover, that " the Lord our God is a consuming fire " (Deut. iv. 24). Not without cause, therefore, does the sinner fear to approach Him lest, " as wax melteth before the fire, so should the wicked perish before the face of God " (Ps. lxvii. 3).

From this, therefore, it ought to appear evident that the Woman pronounced " blessed among women " (Luke i. 28) is not without her proper function : for her also is found something to do in the work of reconciliation. So great a Mediator is Christ that we have need of another to mediate between Him and us, and for this we can find none so well qualified as Mary. A most cruel mediatrix was our mother Eve, through whom the " old serpent " (Apoc. xii. 9) communicated the mortal poison of sin even to the man ; but Mary is faithful, Mary offers the remedy of salvation both to men and women. The former became the means of our seduction, the latter co-operated in our reconciliation ; the former was made the instrument of temptation, the latter the channel of redemption.

Why should human fragility fear to have recourse to Mary ? In her is found nothing austere, nothing to terrify : everything about her is full of sweetness. She has for all only the sweetness of milk and the softness

of wool. Review carefully in your minds the whole of
the Gospel narrative, and if you can discover in Mary
anything at all that appears reproachful or harsh, or
any, even the very least, sign of indignation, look upon
her with suspicion for the future and fear to approach
her. But if, as must really be the fact, you find everything that belongs to her full of goodness and grace, re-
dolent of mercy and meekness : oh, then return thanks
to Him Who, in His compassionate loving-kindness, has
given us such a mediatrix as we cannot possibly distrust. For she has " become all things to all men "
(1 Cor. ix. 22), she has made herself " a debtor to the
wise and to the unwise " (Rom. i. 14). To all she
opens wide the bosom of her mercy so that all may
receive of her fulness (John i. 16) : captives deliverance,
the sick health, the sad consolation, sinners pardon,
the just grace, the angels joy, the whole Blessed Trinity
glory, and the Person of the Son the Substance of His
Human Nature : so that "there is no one that can hide
himself from the heat " of her charity (Ps. xviii. 7).

Does it not seem to you, my dearest brethren, that
she can be considered as the " woman clothed with
the sun " of whom the Beloved Disciple speaks in the
Apocalypse ? I allow that what follows in the prophetic vision obliges us to understand it of the Church
Militant. Nevertheless, as it appears to me, we can
also and not unnaturally understand it of Mary. For
she in truth may be said to have clothed herself with
a second sun. I mean to say : just as the material,
visible sun " riseth upon the good and the bad " (Matt.
v. 45) without making any distinction, so does Mary
show herself full of kindness and sweetness to all and
embraces the necessities of all in the limitless extent

of her compassion, without ever inquiring into antecedent merit or demerit. She is exalted above every
kind of defect ; she beyond all other creatures has risen
over and transcended by a most admirable mode of
elevation whatever is perishable or corruptible, so that
she may be truly said to have the moon—the symbol
of change and instability—under her feet. With regard
to the material moon, you would not consider me to
have said anything very wonderful if I told you that
that was under the feet of her who, as we are obliged
to believe, has been exalted above all the angelic
choirs, above even the Cherubim and the Seraphim.
The moon, however, is wont to be taken as the type
not alone of the defect of corruption but also of human
folly, and is moreover employed not infrequently to
designate the Church on earth : for in its mutability
it bears a resemblance to folly and corruption, and to
the Church Militant in that it shines with borrowed
splendour. Now both these metaphorical moons—if I
may be allowed so to speak—are rightly placed under
the feet of Mary, but in different ways. " The fool
changeth like the moon," as it is written—whilst "the
wise man continueth as the sun " (Ecclus. xxvii. 12).
For the sun possesses steadfast heat and light, whereas
the moon can boast of light alone, and a light that is
extremely inconstant and variable, that " never continueth in the same state " (Job xiv. 2). Not without
reason, therefore, is Mary represented as clothed with
the sun, since she has penetrated the unfathomable
abyss of divine wisdom to a degree that is almost
incredible ; so that we can say of her that she is
immersed in that ocean of inaccessible light as utterly
as is possible to any created nature not deified by

hypostatic union. She is plunged, I say, in that heavenly fire wherewith the Prophet's lips were purified (Is. vi. 6, 7), and wherewith the Seraphim are inflamed.* For Mary has merited far more than the prophets or the Seraphim. To her it is due not merely to be lightly touched with that fire, but to be completely surrounded with it, to be utterly enveloped and absorbed in it. Most intense, undoubtedly, is the light and heat of this Woman's clothing, in whom everything is so beautifully bright and warm that it would be impious to suspect her of containing anything, I do not say darksome, but even obscure or otherwise than perfectly luminous; anything, I do not say tepid, but otherwise than most exceedingly ardent.

The moon of folly, therefore, is so entirely under her feet that she has nothing in common with senseless women and belongs not to the number of foolish virgins. Yea, more : even that first of fools and prince over the whole empire of folly, who, having indeed " changed as the moon," " lost his wisdom in his beauty " (Ezech. xxviii. 17), even he has been trampled and crushed under Mary's heel (Gen. iii. 15), and suffers now a most miserable servitude. For Mary is the Woman, promised of old by God, who should crush the serpent's head with the foot of her virtue, and for whose heel he has lain in wait with many wiles, but all to no purpose (ibid.). It is through Mary alone that every impious heresy has been vanquished.† One heresiarch maintained that Christ, although brought forth by her,

* The Hebrew word " seraph " means to " burn," so that these highest of heavenly spirits owe their name to the burning ardour of their love.—(Translator.)

† Cf. Newman's *Discourses to Mixed Congregations*, pages 367 et sqq.

was not formed from her flesh ; another insisted with serpentine voice (*sibilabat*) that she did not bring forth the Divine Child at all, but only found Him ; a third put forward the blasphemous doctrine that she ceased to be a virgin, at least after the Saviour's birth ; whilst a fourth, unable to endure that she should be called the Mother of God, impiously sought to deprive her of that crowning title.   But the serpents lying in wait have been crushed, the would-be supplanters have been trodden under foot, the slanderers of Mary have been put to confusion and, behold, all generations now call her blessed (Luke i. 48).   Even at the beginning and long before the time of these heretics, the dragon, in the person of King Herod, had lain in wait for the Mother whilst she was about to be delivered, in order to seize and devour her Son (Apoc. xii. 4), because there have always been enmities between the Woman's Seed and the seed of the dragon.

But, my brethren, if you prefer to understand the Church as designated by the name of the moon, because, like the moon, it shines with a borrowed splendour, borrowed from Him Who has said, " Without Me you can do nothing " (John xv. 5) : you have clearly indicated to you the mediatrix of whom I have just been speaking.   " A great sign appeared in heaven," says the Evangelist, " a woman clothed with the sun and the moon under her feet."   O my dearest brethren, let us embrace the feet of Mary, let us prostrate ourselves at those blessed feet in devout supplication.   Let us take hold of her and not let her go until she blesses us (Gen. xxxii. 26), for she surely has the power.   What else is the symbolic fleece placed between the dew and the floor (Judges vi. 37), and the Woman standing

between the sun and the moon, but Mary mediating
between Christ and the Church ?   I suppose the fleece
drenched with the dew does not surprise you so much
as the Woman clothed with the sun.   For certainly
this latter image implies a very intimate relation and
a very close proximity of the Woman to the sun.   How
indeed can a nature so delicate subsist in the midst of
such a consuming fire ?   No wonder, O holy Moses, no
wonder thou art astonished and desirest to examine
this miracle more closely.   Nevertheless, " put off the
shoes from thy feet " (Exod. iii. 5) ; lay aside the
encumbrance of thy carnal thoughts, if thou wishest
to approach.   " I will go," he said, " and see this great
sight " (ibid. 3).   A great sight indeed was that—a
bush burning without being consumed ; a great wonder
also—a Woman clothed with the sun yet suffering no
harm.   It is not in accordance with the nature of a
bush to be entirely surrounded with flames and remain
unburnt ; nor is it possible for a woman of her own
natural strength to endure to be clothed with the sun.
No, this is not the province of human virtue or even
of angelic : something greater is required.   " The Holy
Ghost shall come upon thee," said the Archangel,
speaking to the Virgin (Luke i. 35).   And lest she should
reply that " God is a Spirit " (John iv. 24) and " the
Lord our God a consuming fire " (Deut. iv. 24), he went
on to reassure her : " The power—not my power, nor
thy power—but the power of the Most High shall overshadow thee."   No wonder, then, if under the shelter
of such a divine shadow even a woman can endure to
be clothed with the sun.

" A great sign appeared in heaven : a woman clothed
with the sun."   Yes, in the words of the Psalmist, she

was "clothed with light as with a garment" (Ps. ciii. 2). Perhaps "the sensual man understandeth not" this, because it is spiritual and consequently seems "foolishness to him" (1 Cor. ii. 14). But not so did it seem to the Apostle who recommended his followers to "put on the Lord Jesus Christ" (Rom. xiii. 14). O Lady, how intimate is thy relation with the Sovereign Lord of all ! How near, how closely united to Him thou hast merited to be ! What a fulness of grace thou hast found with Him ! He abideth in thee and thou in Him ; thou clothest Him and art in turn clothed by Him. Thou clothest Him with the substance of thy virginal flesh and He clothes thee in return with the glory of His majesty. Thou clothest the Sun with a cloud and art clothed by the Sun with His splendour. " For the Lord hath created a new thing upon the earth" : that " a woman should compass a man" (Jer. xxxi. 22), and no other man but Christ, of Whom it is said, " Behold a Man, the Orient is His name" (Zach. vi. 12). A new thing hath the Lord created in heaven also : that a woman should appear clothed with the sun. The Mother has crowned the Son and has deserved to be crowned by Him in turn. " Go forth, ye daughters of Sion," says the Holy Spirit in the Canticle, " and see King Solomon in the diadem wherewith His Mother hath crowned Him " * (Cant. iii. 11). But another time for this. Go forth now to see the Queen in the diadem wherewith her Son hath crowned her.

* The Saint elsewhere proposes two explanations of this text : (1) the Mother is Mary and she has crowned her Son, the true Peace-Maker, with the diadem of His Sacred Humanity ; (2) the Mother is the Synagogue and she has crowned her Son, the Messiah, with a crown of thorns —(Translator).

" And on her head a crown of twelve stars." Most worthy of being crowned with a diadem of stars is that august head which, surpassing in splendour all the stars of the firmament, is more an ornament to them than they are to it. And what wonder that she who is clothed with the sun should be crowned with the stars? She is encompassed " as with the flowers of roses in the days of the spring" (Ecclus. l. 8) and as with the lilies of the valleys. For the Bridegroom's " left hand is under her head and with His right He embraces her " (Cant. ii. 6). Who can appraise the jewels that adorn Mary's crown? Who can name the stars that compose her queenly diadem? My brethren, it is beyond the power of any man to say what is the nature of this crown and rightly to explain its constitution.

Far be it from me, therefore, with my very limited capacity, to be so rashly presumptuous as to endeavour to pry into this divine secret. Nevertheless, I think we may, without any impropriety, understand those twelve stars wherewith Mary is singularly adorned as designating twelve grand prerogatives of grace. For we can discover in Mary three kinds of prerogatives, which I will call the prerogatives of heaven, the prerogatives of the flesh, and the prerogatives of the heart. And if now these three constellations be multiplied by four as containing each four stars, we shall have perhaps the twelve stars which make the diadem of our glorious Queen resplendent beyond all others. Now, with regard to the first of our constellations, it seems to me I can discern the brightness of one beautiful star in Mary's generation, of another in the angelic salutation, of a third in the descent of the

Holy Ghost upon her, and of a fourth in her unspeakable conception of the Son of God. So, too, in the second constellation four bright and beautiful stars are plainly visible : her prerogative of being the first of virgins, her virginal fecundity, her easy pregnancy, her painless child-birth. And amongst what I have named the prerogatives of the heart—which constitute our third constellation—we behold shining with dazzling splendour her modest meekness, her devout humility, her magnanimous faith, her interior martyrdom. I will leave it to your own industry to examine each of these stars more particularly. For myself, I think I shall have done sufficient if I am able to point them out in a few words for your pious contemplation.

What, then, is the star which adorns with its splendour the generation of Mary ? Undoubtedly it is the nobility of her descent : for she is sprung from a line of kings, from the seed of Abraham, from the illustrious stock of David. Perhaps this will seem but slight honour. Add to it therefore what is known to you all that she was given by God to her parents and ancestors as the reward of their singular sanctity, that she was promised to the Patriarchs long ages before, that she was foreshadowed in mystical wonders, and heralded from afar in prophetic oracles. For she it is who was prefigured by the rod of Aaron what time it blossomed without roots in the earth (Num. xvii. 8) ; she it is who was typified by Gedeon's fleece, which was found saturated with dew in the midst of the dry thrashing-floor (Judges vi. 37, 38) ; she it is whom the Eastern Gate of Ezechiel's prophetic vision was intended to designate, the gate that was to be opened to no man " because the Lord God of Israel hath

entered in by it " (Ezech. xliv. 2) ; she it is, finally,
who was promised by Isaias, at one time under the
image of the " rod springing forth out of the root of
Jesse " (Is. xi. 1), at another more clearly as the
Virgin that should bear a Son (Is. vii. 14).   Justly,
therefore, is it said with reference to this prodigy of
the Woman clothed with the sun that " a great sign
appeared in heaven " (Apoc. xii. 1), since, as you know,
it was promised from heaven long ages before it was
seen upon earth.   " The Lord Himself shall give you a
sign," said the Prophet, " Behold a Virgin shall conceive and bear a Son " (Is. vii. 14).   Great in truth is
the sign He has given us because He Who has given
it is Himself so great.   What created eye can contemplate the glory of this unique prerogative without
being dazzled and blinded with the excess of its
splendour ?   The very fact that she was saluted with
so much reverence and humility by the Archangel
that he seemed to have beheld her already on her
royal throne, exalted above all the shining ranks of the
heavenly host, and to have all but worshipped this
daughter of Adam—he who had been accustomed
hitherto to receive the willingly-accorded worship of
men : this very fact, I say, is sufficient to show us
how surpassing is the merit of our own glorious Virgin
and how singular her grace.

Bright too is the glory of her unparalleled motherhood.   For not in iniquity did Mary conceive her Son
—in this unlike all other mothers (Ps. l. 7) : she alone
amongst women conceived through the operation of
grace and by the power of the Holy Spirit.   And He
Whom she brought forth is true God and the true Son
of God, so that the Child Who was born of the Virgin

is at the same time the Son of God and the Son of man, at the same time true God and true Man : here, my brethren, you have a very abyss of light, the dazzling refulgence of which I can hardly believe it possible for even the angelic eye to endure. Besides, that which rendered particularly illustrious both the integrity of her flesh and her vow of virginity was the very novelty of her holy purpose : because, namely, in liberty of spirit going beyond all the prescriptions of the Mosaic Law, she consecrated her virginity to God by vow, that she might be spotlessly " holy in body and in spirit " (1 Cor. vii. 34). And she proved the immovable firmness of her resolve by the constancy of will implied in her answer to the Angel's promise of a son : " How shall this be done because I know not man ? " (Luke i. 34). Likely enough, the reason why she was at first troubled at the greeting of Gabriel " and thought within herself what manner of salutation this might be " (ibid. 29) was the fact that he pronounced her " blessed among women," whereas it had ever been her wish to be blessed among virgins. Consequently, on hearing from the Angel the words, " Blessed art thou among women," she " thought within herself what manner of salutation this might be," for it seemed to her to have a suspicious sound. But the moment the danger to her virginity appeared manifest in the promise of a son, she could no longer conceal her alarm and said, " How shall this be done, because I know not man ? " Deservedly therefore, did she obtain the one blessing without forfeiting the other, so that her virginity derived a great increase of glory from her fruitfulness and her fruitfulness in like manner was enhanced by her virginity : as two stars that seem to borrow additional brightness from each other's rays. For it is doubtless a grand thing to be a virgin ; but to be a virgin and a mother at once—that is something far greater and grander in every way.

Deservedly also was she alone spared that trial of extreme lassitude from which all other mothers suffer during the period of gestation, because she alone conceived without any experience of carnal delight. Hence, at the very beginning of her pregnancy, when other women are most grievously afflicted, we find Mary ascending the mountains with all alacrity in order to minister to her cousin Elizabeth (Luke i. 39).   We read egain how she went up from Galilee to Bethlehem on the very eve of her child-birth, bearing that most precious Deposit, bearing that most light Burden, bearing Him by Whom she was herself borne.   And with regard to her child-birth, how brilliant a star is that which shines out in the unparalleled exultation wherewith she brought forth her unparalleled Offspring, exempted alone amongst women from the common curse and pain that belong to parturition ! If we are to estimate the value of things from their rarity, these prerogatives must be held in highest esteem, since surely nothing more rare can be found. For truly with respect to them all Mary

> Had no precursor in the years before
> And peerless shall remain for evermore — SEDULIUS.

And for ourselves, dearest brethren, if we contemplate by the light of faith these glorious privileges of the Virgin Mother, they will be sure to arouse in us sentiments of admiration, veneration, and devotion, yea, and will impart to us no little consolation.

But the wonders whereof it remains to speak have to

be imitated as well as admired. As concerns the preceding, it was not given to any of us to be promised by God or announced from heaven long before our birth " at sundry times and in divers manners " (Heb. i. 1), nor to receive from the mouth of the Archangel Gabriel the honour of so unusual a salutation : much less can we pretend to a participation in the two others, with regard to which the Virgin seems to say like the Prophet, " My secret to myself, my secret to myself " (Is. xxiv. 16). For she is the only one of whom it has ever been said, " That Which is conceived in her is of the Holy Ghost " (Matt. i. 20) ; she is the only one to whom it has ever been said, " The Holy Which shall be born of thee shall be called the Son of God " (Luke i. 35). By all means, let other " virgins be brought to the King," but let it be " after her " (Ps. xliv. 15) ; for she claims the first place for herself alone. Much more is she solitary in her privilege of conceiving without corruption, of bearing without weariness, and of bringing forth without pain. Consequently, my brethren, nothing of these things is required of us. But there are certain other things which are required. For should any of us be found wanting in the meekness of modesty, or in humility of heart, or in greatness and constancy of faith, or in compassion of soul : think you we shall be able to justify our negligence by pleading that these gifts like the others are singular in Mary ? No, my brethren, most assuredly we shall not. Undoubtedly, the blush on the face of a modest man is a most lovely jewel in his diadem, a most beautiful star on his brow.*

* Cf. the Saint's beautiful Sermon on Modesty, the last of the series on the Canticle of Canticles.

And how can anyone suppose that this grace was
wanting to her who was full of grace ? (Luke i. 28).
Oh, yes, Mary was modest in the highest degree.
This can be proved from the Gospel. For where
does she ever appear garrulous ?   Where do we ever
find her in the least degree presumptuous ?   She was
content to stand outside the door, seeking a word
with her Son, when in virtue of her authority as His
Mother she might have unceremoniously entered the
house where Jesus was preaching and interrupted the
sermon (Matt. xii. 46).   In the whole text of the four
Gospels — unless my memory plays me false — Mary can
be heard speaking not oftener than four times.   The
first occasion is where she answered the Angel, but
only after she had been addressed by him once and
again.   The second is where she spoke to Elizabeth, in
whose womb the voice of her salutation had made the
unborn Baptist to leap for joy, and whilst the mother
of John was magnifying Mary, Mary's sole solicitude
was to magnify the Lord (Luke i. 40-46).   The third
is where she complained to her Son, when He was now
twelve years of age, that she and His father had been
seeking Him sorrowing (Luke ii. 48).   The fourth is
where she spoke to Jesus and the waiters at the
wedding-feast (John ii. 3-5).   Her words on this last
occasion gave signal proof of her natural meekness
and virginal modesty.   For esteeming as her own the
embarrassment of her neighbour, she could not rest
easy, neither could she forbear speaking to her Son of
the failure of the wine.   And on being apparently reproved by Him, she showed how " meek and humble
of heart " (Matt. xi. 29) she was by answering never a
word, yet without losing confidence, since she said to

the waiters, " Whatsoever He shall say to you, do ye "
(John ii. 5).

Have you not read how in the beginning, when the
shepherds came to Bethlehem, Mary was the first to
meet them ?   " They came with haste," says the
Evangelist, " and they found Mary and Joseph, and
the Infant lying in the manger " (Luke ii. 16).   So
also with the Magi, as you will remember : they found
the Child, but not without His Mother (Matt. ii. 11).
And when Mary was bringing the Lord of the temple
into the temple of the Lord, she heard much concerning Him from holy Simeon, much also that concerned
herself, being " swift to hear but slow to speak "
(James i. 19) ; and we are told that she " kept all these
words, pondering them in her heart " (Luke ii. 19).
But on none of these occasions was she heard to utter
a single syllable about the glorious mystery of the
Lord's incarnation.   Woe unto us " whose soul is in
our nostrils " (Is. ii. 22) !   Woe unto us who imitate
the fool that " uttereth all his mind " (Prov. xxix. 11) !
Woe unto us

> Whose words flow out as unrestrained
> As water through a sieve.*

How often Mary heard her Son not only speaking
to the multitude in parables (Matt. xiii. 34), but revealing to His disciples apart the mysteries of the
kingdom of God !   She saw Him working miracles, she
saw Him hanging on the cross, she saw Him expiring
in torments, she saw Him rising from the tomb, she
saw Him lastly mounting up to heaven.   But how
seldom in the records of all these wonders do we find

* " Pleni rimarum effluimus undique " (Terence, *Eunocho*,
I. ii. 25).

it mentioned that the voice of this most modest Virgin, of this most chaste Turtle-Dove was heard! Again, we read in the Acts of the Apostles how, after returning from the Mount of Olives, " all were persevering with one mind in prayer." Who? Surely if Mary happened to be present she must be mentioned first, for she is over all other creatures, both on account of her Son's Divine dignity and by reason of the merit of her personal holiness. Yet what do we find? " Peter and John, James and Andrew, Philip and Thomas, Bartholomew and Matthew, James of Alpheus and Simon Zelotes, and Jude, the brother of James : all these were persevering with one mind in prayer with the women and Mary the Mother of Jesus " (Acts i. 13, 14). You see, my brethren, how she made herself the last even of the women, so that she might occupy the last place of all. The apostles were indeed still carnally-minded— " for as yet the Spirit was not given to them because Jesus was not yet glorified " (John vii. 39) — when " there arose a strife amongst them as to which of them should seem to be greater " (Luke xxii. 24), whilst Mary, in proportion as she surpassed all, humbled herself in all things, yea and regarded herself as the least of all. Rightly, therefore, was she from last made first who, whereas she was the greatest of all, had made herself the least of all (Matt. xx. 16). Rightly was she made mistress of all who conducted herself as the handmaid of all. And rightly was she exalted above the angels, who in her unutterable modesty and meekness had placed herself below widows and penitents, even below her from whom seven devils had been cast out (Luke viii. 2). O my dearest children, have zeal, I beg of you, have zeal for this virtue of meekness, if you love Mary ; if you desire to please Mary neglect not to imitate her modesty. For there is nothing more becoming a man, nothing more proper for a Christian, above all, nothing more befitting a monk.

Now with regard to the Virgin's humility, that virtue shines forth clearly enough from her meekness. These two virtues of humility and meekness are foster-sisters, suckled at the same breast, nay, they have been united yet more intimately in Him Who said, " Learn of Me because I am meek and humble of heart " (Matt. xi. 29). And just as pride is the mother of presumption, so it is only from sincere humility that true meekness can come.   It is not, however, in her silence alone that Mary's humility is manifest : it appears more evidently still in her words. She heard the announcement, " The Holy Which shall be born of thee shall be called the Son of God," and her only answer was : " Behold the handmaid of the Lord " (Luke ii. 38) ! She then set out on a journey to visit her cousin Elizabeth, to whom the Virgin's incomparable glory was revealed by the Holy Spirit Himself ; so that, over-awed by the dignity of Mary, she cried out, " Whence is this to me that the Mother of my Lord should come to me ? " (ibid. 43). She also acknowledged the power of grace in the voice that saluted her, by adding, " As soon as the voice of thy salutation sounded in my ears, the infant in my womb leaped for joy " (ibid. 44). And she commended the faith of Mary when she said, " Blessed art thou that hast believed, because those things shall be accomplished that were spoken to thee by the Lord " (ibid. 45). Magnificent eulogiums indeed ! But the Virgin's devout humility would allow her to keep nothing for herself. All was referred to Him Whose gifts were being praised in her. " Thou dost magnify me, the Mother of the Lord," so she says in effect in answer to her cousin, " but ' my soul doth magnify the Lord.' Thou sayest that at the sound of my voice the infant in thy womb leaped for joy, but ' my spirit hath rejoiced in God my Saviour ' (ibid. 46, 47). Yea and if thy unborn infant, as ' the friend of the Bridegroom, rejoiceth with joy,' it is ' because of the Bridegroom's voice ' (John iii. 29). Thou pronouncest me blessed for having believed, but the one cause both of my belief and of my blessedness is the regard of the Sovereign Goodness, so that if ' from henceforth all generations shall call me blessed ' it is only ' because He hath regarded the humility of His handmaid ' (Luke i. 48)."

But, brethren, are we to suppose that St. Elizabeth erred in what she uttered under the inspiration of the Spirit of God ? Heaven forbid ! Blessed assuredly was she whom the Lord had regard to and blessed also she that believed. In fact, we can say that Mary's heroic faith was the noble fruit of the divine regard. For by an unutterable artifice — if the expression may be allowed — of the Holy Spirit Who came down upon her, such magnanimity of faith was united in the secret chamber of the Virgin's heart to such profound humility that — as I have said of the union of integrity with motherhood — these two stars also received additional brightness from each other's rays. That is to say : her abysmal humility did not diminish the magnanimity of her faith, nor did the latter prejudice the former ; but whilst remaining the humblest of all in her conceit of herself, she showed herself most magnanimous by her faith in the divine promise : she, who considered herself nothing better than a poor little handmaid, believed, nevertheless, with the most undoubting faith, that she was chosen by the Lord for the accomplishment of His incomprehensible design of becoming man, chosen for that most " admirable intercourse,"* chosen to co-operate in that unsearchable mystery ; and she was firmly persuaded that she would soon be verily and indeed the Mother of the God-Man.   It is the prerogative of divine grace to be able to work this double miracle in the hearts of the elect : that humility shall not make them pusillanimous, nor magnanimity render them proud, but rather that these two virtues shall assist and enhance one another.   Thus it comes about that not only no self-elation results from magnanimity but, contrariwise, humility is thereby best promoted, for men are found to be distrustful of self and grateful to their Divine Benefactor in proportion as they are magnanimous ; on the other hand, likewise, the virtue of humility does not make a man faint-hearted, but on the contrary, the less one is wont to presume on his own powers, even in the smallest things, the greater shall be his reliance on the help of God in matters more important.

The † martyrdom of Mary – which, if you remember, I have enumerated in the twelfth and last place amongst the stars of her diadem — we find recorded for us both in the prophecy of Simeon and in the story

* Words taken from the first antiphon for Vespers of the Feast of Circumcision.

† This and the following paragraph are used for the lessons of the second nocturn on the Feast of the Seven Dolours, kept in the Cistercian Order on the Friday before Palm Sunday — (Translator).

of the Lord's passion. "Behold," said the holy old man, speaking of the Infant Jesus, "this Child is set for a sign which shall be contradicted, and thine own soul," he added, addressing the Mother, "a sword shall pierce" (Luke ii. 34, 35). Truly, O blessed Mother, truly did the iron pierce thy soul (Ps. civ. 18), for it could not otherwise pierce the Flesh of thy Son. After the death of thy Jesus—thy Jesus, I say, because although common to all of us He is in an especial manner thine —His Soul could not be wounded by the cruel lance that opened His side—not sparing Him even in death Whom it was no longer capable of hurting—but thy soul, O Mary, it could and did transpierce. For His Soul no longer occupied His now lifeless Heart, whence thy soul could by no means be withdrawn. Consequently thy soul was transfixed with the violence of sorrow, so that thou art justly proclaimed to be more than a martyr, since the sufferings thou didst endure from the force of thy compassion far exceeded all the pains that could have been inflicted on thy flesh.

"Woman, behold thy son" (John xix. 26). Poor Mother! Were not these words to thee as the sharpest of swords, piercing thy soul "and reaching unto the division of the soul and the spirit" (Heb. iv. 12)? Oh, what an exchange! John is given thee in place of Jesus, the servant in place of the Lord, the disciple for the Master, the son of Zebedee instead of the Son of God, a mere man instead of Him Who is true and very God! Oh, how the sound of those words must have pierced through thy most affectionate heart, since even the very remembrance of them is enough to break these stony, these iron hearts of ours! Wonder not, dearest brethren, that Mary is said to have suffered martyrdom in her soul. He alone ought to be surprised at this whosoever does not remember to have heard St. Paul mentioning amongst the worst crimes of the Gentiles that they were " without affection " (Rom. i. 31). Far removed from such a vice was the heart of Mary, and far removed from it also be the hearts of us, her poor servants. But perchance some one will say to me, " Did not Mary know beforehand that her Son was doomed to die " ? Undoubtedly. " Did she not hope that He would speedily arise again from the tomb " ? Most firmly. "And nevertheless, in spite of this foreknowledge and this expectation did she sorrow over her crucified Son " ? Yea, and with a sorrow exceeding great. Let me ask thee, who art thou, my brother, and whence hast thou derived this wisdom that thou shouldst marvel more at Mary's compassion than at the passion of her Son ? Dost thou grant that He could die even the death of the body, and yet deny her the power of participating in His death by the affections of her heart ? The Son's death of pain was caused by love greater than which no man hath (John xv. 13), and the Mother's death of sympathy was caused by love the like of which was never felt before in the heart of a pure creature.

O Mother of mercy, the Moon, that is, the Church on earth, prostrate at thy sacred feet, implores of thee, her appointed Advocate with the Divine Sun of Justice, implores of thee with devout supplication and by all the affections of thy most pure heart, that thou wouldst obtain for her the grace " in thy light to see the light " (Ps. xxxv. 10), that thou wouldst conciliate for her the favour of thy Son Who loves thee and has adorned thee beyond all others, investing thee with a "robe of glory" (Ecclus. vi. 32) and setting "a crown of beauty upon thy head" (Ezech. xvi. 12). Thou, O Virgin, art full of all grace, full of the dew of heaven, "flowing with delights, leaning upon thy Beloved" (Cant. viii. 5). Feed us to-day, O great Lady, feed us, thy poor mendicants, with the food of the spirit; let "the whelps also eat of the crumbs that fall from thy table" (Matt. xv. 27); give not alone Abraham's servant but his camels also to drink from thy overflowing pitcher (Gen. xxiv. 18, 19), because thou art the true Rebecca chosen and pre-destined for the Son of the Most High, Jesus Christ our Lord, Who is over all things, God blessed for ever. Amen.